A Cook's Calendar
From Agnes Toms

—School and work lunches for *September*
—*October's* brightness calls for hearty break-
fasts
—Holiday feasting in *November*
—Christmas cheer in *December* with gifts
from the kitchen
—Hearty soups for *January*
—In *February* a flair for fabulous fish
—New ways for vegetables in *March*
—Eggs, Easter and other, for *April*
—Sweeten *May* with honey dishes
—*June* is dairy month
—Outdoor eating and family fun in *July*
—Zesty salads for *August*

Agnes Toms

Natural Foods
Meals & Menus
For All Seasons

Keats Publishing, Inc.   New Canaan, Connecticut

Also by Agnes Toms:

Delicious and Nutritious

Eat, Drink and Be Healthy

**Natural Foods MEALS AND MENUS
FOR ALL SEASONS**

Pivot edition published 1973

Copyright © 1973 by Agnes Toms

All Rights Reserved

Printed in the United States of America

Library of Congress Catalog Card Number: 73-75086

PIVOT ORIGINAL HEALTH BOOKS are published
by Keats Publishing, Inc., 212 Elm Street,
New Canaan, Connecticut   06840

Dedicated to my Granddaughter

PATRICIA TERRELL

*whose perfect little body is
the result of her Grandmother's teaching*

CONTENTS

Acknowledgments

The author wishes to thank those loyal friends who urged her to write this book.

She is also very grateful to Norman Bassett, Dr. Joe Nichols, Tom Lavin, and the American Nutrition Society, for permitting her to use recipes first written for their magazines.

Thanks also go to Linda Clark for her encouragement; to Merle Peterson for typing the manuscript and to Margaret Dutcher who edited the manuscipt.

The increasing popular interest in Natural foods has prompted me to select these recipes from among those I have published over a period of years in such magazines as *Let's Live*, *Natural Foods and Farming* and *Modern Nutrition*.

Each month in these magazines I featured recipes that were particularly applicable and obtainable for each season of the year. In this way the reader had recipes for fresh, unprocessed foods as they would appear in season at the markets. Included with these recipes are those for special occasions and holidays such as Thanksgiving, Christmas and Easter.

Although modern methods of processing foods have almost eliminated seasonal buying, there are still many people who prefer to eat food that is unprocessed and which comes garden fresh as it is in season.

Because food is one of the most important needs of life and has a direct influence on our health we should be vitally interested in preparing fresh and naturally produced food. To paraphrase the old proverb, "all things have their season."

AGNES TOMS

September

THE LUNCH BOX

THE LUNCH BOX

In four out of ten homes someone carries a lunch to work or school almost every day. Also, in four out of ten homes, someone probably says, "What shall I pack for lunch today?" The homemaker who packs lunches, day in and day out for members of her family faces a real challenge.

A work lunch that is more than a sandwich is the meal which must give renewed energy and vigor for the afternoon's work.

A favorite salad (see August chapter), a hot dish packed in a wide-mouth vacuum bottle, and some cold meat and cheese is an appealing and nourishing combination. Pack salads in wide-mouth screw-top jars. Raw vegetable salads should be first choice, but some cooked vegetable salads such as Three Bean Salad run a close second.

In the vacuum bottle, put hot soup or a leftover casserole dish (see January chapter). Be sure to scald the inside of your thermos with boiling water before filling. This will help to keep the contents hot.

Cold meat or cheese should be packed in a tight, air-free wrapper. Cold chicken, chunks of stew meat or roast beef from the previous night's dinner are favorites of lunch-carrying men. When there is no leftover meat they may take wedges of natural cheese or pieces of cooked fish.

These foods may be accompanied by bread-and-butter sandwiches made of any wholegrain bread. Vary the usual butter by using spreads made of nut butters such as peanut, almond, cashew, etc. Nut or seed butters can be ground in your blender or seed mill.

Tuck in a snack for the traditional coffee break. This can be finger-food such as dates or prunes stuffed with nuts, a handful of raisins and nuts, cracked nuts, chunks of cheese, a piece of fresh coconut or fresh fruit or vegetable.

School lunches for young children can be less varied than the work lunch, but they should please the taste of each youngster and also contain about one-third of his daily food requirement.

Put plenty of fruit in his lunch box, and include one-half pint of milk in a thermos bottle if the school does not have a milk program. Make sandwiches with protein filling, such as cheese, meat, eggs, fish or nut butters. Use a variety of wholegrain breads, such as rye, wheat, oatmeal, soya and corn meal.

Here are some other suggestions:

Make sandwiches ahead of time and freeze them. Place the wrapped frozen sandwiches in the lunch box. They will thaw out by noon.

To prepare sandwiches for freezing, butter bread, muffins or rolls to the edge. Place a thin layer of salad dressing over the butter. Place slices of ham, turkey, beef, tuna mixtures or nut butter between the slices. Wrap sandwiches individually in plastic wrap, then wrap in foil and freeze. When preparing the lunch, wrap lettuce separately in plastic wrap, to be added to sandwiches at school.

When the weather is cold, fill a thermos with the child's favorite soup. Canned or frozen fruit is a nice change from an apple or orange. Pack the fruit in plastic dishes that seal well.

Do not put in large apples or oranges or large pieces of other fruit. As a lunchroom supervisor for many years, I learned that children either do not attempt to eat a large apple or eat only part of it in their rush to get through lunch and out to the playground.

Stuff celery sticks with peanut butter, cream cheese, whipped cottage cheese with chopped nuts and mashed Cheddar cheese and chopped olives.

Make a salad on a stick, using a meat skewer. Include cherry tomatoes, celery slices, tiny cooked beets, carrot slices and Cheddar cheese chunks. You can do a similar thing with pineapple chunks, mild cheese cubes and any dried fruit.

Have popped corn on hand for lunch boxes or for the after-school snack. It is easy to pop corn perfectly. Warm the popper (or a heavy pan) and put in one-fourth cup of oil. When the oil is hot, drop in a test kernel or two. Then, when these begin to spin, it is time to pour in enough kernels to cover the bottom of the pan, put on the lid, and shake the pan gently until the popping stops. Salt or not, according to your taste.

If you find that many kernels fail to pop, it is probably due to lack of moisture. Add 2 tablespoons of water to each pound of corn. Shake the corn and let it stand for 2 or 3 days before using. Corn should be kept in an airtight container in a cool place.

SANDWICH SUGGESTIONS

1. Rye bread—liver sausage, ham or tongue
2. Wholewheat breads—tuna, egg salad or meatloaf
3. Boston Brown bread—baked beans and finely chopped onion
4. Oatmeal bread—chicken and chopped celery
5. Cracked wheat bread—cottage cheese with grated raw carrot
6. Soya bread—peanut butter with bananas or apple, never jelly or honey

7. Onion bread—Cheddar cheese and sliced tomatoes
8. Pumpernickel bread—corned beef
9. Meat and cheese stacks—no bread used
10. Sweet breads—cream cheese with nuts

These are only a few suggestions. Some popular
filling recipes follow:

EGG SALAD FILLING FOR 8 SANDWICHES

Combine:

*6 hard-boiled eggs,
chopped*
⅔ cup finely chopped celery

¼ cup salad dressing
*1 tablespoon prepared
mustard*
½ teaspoon salt

TUNA SALAD FILLING FOR 6 SANDWICHES

Combine:

*1 can (6½ ounces) chunk
style tuna, drain and
rinse in hot water then
flake*
2 hard-boiled eggs chopped

¾ cup finely chopped celery
*¼ cup chopped pickle
(optional)*
½ cup mayonnaise

CORNED BEEF FILLING FOR 6 SANDWICHES

Combine:

*1½ cups chopped corned
beef*
½ cup diced celery
2 teaspoons grated onion

*4 teaspoons prepared
mustard*
2 tablespoons mayonnaise

PEANUT BUTTER CARROT FILLING

*¾ cup (not homogenized)
peanut butter*
2 tablespoons mayonnaise

*1½ cups finely grated
carrots or alfalfa sprouts*

Blend above ingredients. Makes about 2½ cups.

CHEESE AND CABBAGE FILLING

½ cup finely shredded
  cabbage
2 tablespoons shredded
  cheddar cheese

1 tablespoon minced green
  pepper
1 tablespoon chili sauce

Mix ingredients well. Makes ½ cup filling.

SPROUT SANDWICHES

Spread thin slices of wholegrain bread with a butter-oil mixture. (Blend ½ cup butter with ⅛ cup salad oil.) Cover spread with cream cheese and a generous amount of alfalfa sprouts. Cover with buttered top slice. Serves 8-10.

PICKLED EGGS

6 hard-boiled eggs
¾ cup liquid drained from
  cooked beets
¾ cup vinegar

1 bay leaf
¾ teaspoon salt
Dash of pepper
1 clove garlic, crushed

Shell eggs and place in a quart jar. Combine beet liquid, vinegar, bay leaf, salt, pepper and garlic. Heat but do not boil. Pour over eggs. Cool, then cover and refrigerate overnight or longer. Serves 6.

GOURMET CHICKEN SANDWICHES

1 cup chopped cooked
  chicken (or tuna)
½ cup finely chopped crisp
  celery
½ cup finely chopped
  cucumber

¼ cup chopped walnuts
⅛ teaspoon salt
⅓ cup salad dressing
Wholegrain bread

Combine chicken with celery, cucumber, nuts and salt. Add only enough salad dressing to moisten. Spread bread slices with softened butter. Use about 3 teaspoons of sandwich filling for each sandwich. Serves 10-12.

TURKEY AND CRESS SANDWICHES

Combine 2 cups chopped cooked turkey meat with 2 cups watercress leaves (no stems) and ¾ cup mayonnaise. Season with salt to taste and ¼ cup minced celery. Spread on buttered wholewheat bread. Makes 6 to 8 sandwiches.

CURRIED EGG SALAD SANDWICH

Another tasty way to use up hard-boiled eggs.

Combine ½ cup chopped pimiento-stuffed olives, ½ cup mayonnaise, 6 chopped hard-boiled eggs, ½ teaspoon curry powder, salt and pepper to taste. Mix well and spread on buttered wholegrain bread slices. Top with fresh lettuce leaves and remaining bread slice. Makes 2 cups spread.

BUTTER SPREADS

Have 2 cubes of butter at room temperature. Put in blender and slowly add ⅔ cup vegetable or seed oil (not olive oil). When completely blended press into small square pan and refrigerate until hard. Take out just enough for one meal at a time.

TO MAKE YOUR OWN NUT BUTTER

You can make nut butter from untoasted or toasted nuts, salted or unsalted, blanched or unblanched, each is quite different.

The best butters for spreads and fillings are made from almonds, peanuts, filberts and pine nuts.

English walnuts, black walnuts and pecans are more suitable for butters used in cooking; their astringent flavor becomes too pronounced for just eating unless blended with other ingredients such as butter.

To extend the nut butter you can whip in as much as a double measure of soft butter and chill until firm; this is a good way to make some of the more expensive nuts go further.

Basic nut butter: place 1½ cups whole or broken nuts in a blender. Add salad oil (if nuts are untoasted add 2 extra teaspoons to each amount).

Almonds: add 2 tablespoons oil

Filberts: add 5-6 tablespoons oil

Pistachios: add 1½ tablespoons oil

Pine nuts: add 3 tablespoons oil

Walnuts: add 3-4 tablespoons oil

Pecans: add 3 tablespoons oil

Peanuts need little oil, add only if ground peanuts seem dry.

Since the nut mixture is very thick, make only small batches at one time (such as ½ cup of nuts at a time), so as not to overtax the blender.

When using grinder, use the blade for crushing and put through 2 or 3 times. Add salt to taste.

Keep butters in covered jars in the refrigerator. They become rancid quickly if left at room temperatures. Also, the oil might separate.

SPREADS YOU CAN MAKE AHEAD AND CHILL

Blend equal parts softened butter and cream

cheese; moisten with a little cooked salad dressing. Use plain or blend in:

1. Chopped olives.
2. Equal parts finely diced celery and grated raw carrot, seasoned with salt and pepper.
3. Grated onion, chopped almonds, and a dash of curry powder.
4. Mashed cooked liver and chopped celery; season with a little sour cream and prepared mustard.
5. Grate equal parts Cheddar cheese and Swiss cheese (or put through food chopper); moisten with cottage cheese and sprinkle with caraway seeds.
6. Chop hard-boiled eggs with crisp bacon pieces (or finely chopped celery). Blend in sour cream and a dash of curry.

SANDWICHES YOU CAN FREEZE

1. Ground roast beef, lamb or chicken, moistened with mayonnaise and seasoned with grated onion.
2. Chopped cooked chicken livers or calf liver mixed with mashed hard-boiled egg yolk, minced onion and homemade ketchup.
3. Cream cheese, chopped olives and salted peanuts moistened with salad dressing.
4. Sliced roast lamb, on wholewheat bread spread with mint-seasoned butter. (Cream ¼ pound butter with 1 tablespoon fresh mint.)
5. Peanut butter and applesauce or peanut butter and sliced pickle.
6. Chopped cooked chicken, chopped salted almonds and cream cheese.

WHOLEWHEAT BREAD

1 cup warm water   1 tablespoon honey
2 heaping tablespoons
  yeast or 2 cakes

Put the above into a quart container, mix well and set aside to start rising. Heat 1 cup milk to lukewarm. Into large bowl put the following:

⅔ cup safflower oil   ½ cup honey
  Add the warm milk   2 well-beaten eggs
1 tablespoon salt   yeast mixture

Stir well. Add 8 cups wholewheat flour (pastry). Let rise double, punch down and knead. Let rise in oiled bread pans. Bake at 325°, 45-50 minutes. Makes 2 loaves.

GERMINATED WHEAT BREAD

1 pint clean wheat (obtain   2 tablespoons salt
  from health food store)   2 cups water from soaked
2 tablespoons dry active   wheat
  yeast softened in water to   1½ cups wholewheat flour
  cover   with
2 tablespoons honey or   ½ cup rye flour (optional)
  molasses   OR
2 tablespoons soy lecithin   2 cups wholewheat flour
  or salad oil

Pick over and wash wheat; soak in water to cover for about 18 hours. The water may have a slight smell, but it is all right. Save this water. Grind the soaked germinated wheat with a medium food grinder blade. This will form a soft dough. Put the soft dough in a 2 quart bowl. Add softened yeast, honey or raw sugar, salt, soy lecithin and the 2 cups of warmed drained-off water. Stir in enough flour to make a stiff batter that can be stirred with a large wooden spoon. Cover and place in a warm place until double in size.

Knead on floured board until dough is smooth and heavy. Shape into loaves. Put into greased pans. Place in warm place to rise until pans are full. Heat oven to 350°, then slide loaves gently into oven—bread may fall if it is jolted. Bake 1 hour until brown. Remove from pans onto a wire rack. Butter the outsides for a soft crust. Delicious served warm with herb butter. When toasting this bread, use broiler with slow fire.

This recipe makes 1 loaf 9½ x 5½ by 2½ inches deep; or 2 loaves 7½ x 3½ by 2¼ inches deep. Double the recipe for 4 loaves.

CARROT BREAD

2 cups wholewheat pastry flour	¼ cup nut meats, chopped
1 teaspoon soda	1 cup oil
1 teaspoon baking powder	1 teaspoon vanilla
2 teaspoons cinnamon	½ cup brown sugar
½ teaspoon salt	2 cups grated carrots
1 cup raisins	3 eggs, beaten

Sift flour, soda, baking powder, cinnamon and salt together. Mix all ingredients carefully. Pour into a well-oiled 9x5x3 inch loaf pan. Let stand about 20 minutes before baking. Bake at 350°, for about 1 hour. Cool before slicing to prevent crumbling.

SPOON BREAD

2 cups milk	1 teaspoon salt
½ cup whole cornmeal	3 egg yolks, beaten
1 teaspoon baking powder	3 tablespoons melted butter
1 tablespoon honey	3 egg whites

Heat 2 cups milk to near boiling. Slowly stir in corn-meal. Cook until thick. Remove from fire, add baking powder, honey, salt, beaten egg yolks and melted butter. Fold in well-beaten whites of eggs. Place in buttered casserole and bake at 325°, for 25 minutes. Serve from casserole.

NO-KNEAD BREAD ROLLS

1 cake yeast or 1 package dry yeast	2 tablespoons honey
¼ cup lukewarm water	1 cup boiling water
¼ cup butter or oil	1 egg
1¼ teaspoons salt	2½ cups unbleached white flour

Dissolve yeast cake in lukewarm water. Put butter, salt and honey in separate bowl. Add boiling water and stir until dissolved. When lukewarm, add yeast, then beaten egg. Stir in flour to make soft dough.

Grease large bowl and put dough into it. Cover with buttered plate. Chill 2-3 hours. When ready to use, pinch off little balls and let rise in warm place for 2 hours. Bake in hot oven (425°), for 12 minutes. Makes 2 dozen rolls.

BLUEBERRY MUFFINS

3 tablespoons oil	½ teaspoon salt
1 egg, beaten	3 teaspoons baking powder
¾ cup milk	1 cup fresh or well-drained blueberries
3 tablespoons honey	
2 cups wholewheat flour	

Heat oven to 400°. Combine oil, egg, milk and honey. Sift flour, measure again and sift with salt and baking powder. Add to first mixture with blueberries. Stir only enough to mix. (Over-stirring makes holes in muffins). Fill 12 greased muffin wells. Optional: sprinkle tops lightly with raw sugar. Bake 20 to 30 minutes. Test by pressing lightly on top; if dough springs back, they are done.

DATE APRICOT BREAD

1 cup honey	¼ cup salad oil
½ cup boiling water	1 cup milk
½ cup sliced dried apricots	3 cups unbleached flour
1 cup fresh California dates, diced	3 teaspoons baking powder (tartrate)
1 cup walnuts, chopped	1 teaspoon salt
1 egg	½ teaspoon vanilla

Combine honey, boiling water, apricots and dates. Allow to stand until cool. Add walnuts. In a mixing bowl, beat egg slightly, add oil and milk. Fold in prepared fruit and sifted dry ingredients. Mix only until dry ingredients are blended. Add vanilla. Pour batter into oiled, lined 10x5x3 inch loaf pan. Let stand 15 minutes. Bake at 350° (moderate) about 1¼ hours. Cool in pan 5 minutes, remove paper and cool on wire rack.

ORANGE NUT BREAD

2¼ cups rolled oats, ground in blender or food mill	¾ cup chopped nuts
4 teaspoons baking powder	2 tablespoons oil
¼ teaspoon baking soda	⅔ cup orange juice
¾ teaspoon salt	1 tablespoon orange rind, grated
⅔ cup honey	

Mix dry ingredients thoroughly. Add honey, nuts, oil, orange juice and rind. Stir until dry ingredients are well moistened. Pour into oiled 9x5 inch loaf pan. Bake at 350°, 60 minutes or until firm to touch. To prevent the top from cracking, cover with a hood of aluminum foil (do not touch batter) for the first 20 minutes of baking.

CRANBERRY FRUIT BREAD

2 cups sifted wholewheat flour (pastry)
2 teaspoons baking powder (tartrate)
½ teaspoon soda
1 teaspoon salt
1 cup honey
1 egg, beaten
½ cup orange juice
1 tablespoon grated orange peel
¼ cup oil
½ cup chopped nuts
2 cups cranberries, coarsely chopped

Sift together flour, baking powder, soda and salt. Combine honey, egg, orange juice, peel and oil. Make a well in the dry ingredients and add egg mixture all at once. Mix only to dampen. Carefully fold in nuts and cranberries. Spoon into greased 9x5x3 inch loaf pan. Spread corners and sides slightly higher than center. Bake at 350°, 1 hour or until crust is brown and toothpick inserted comes out clean. Remove from pan.

CRANBERRY BREAD

1 cup raw cranberries
1 cup raw sugar
3 cups sifted unbleached flour
4 teaspoons baking powder (tartrate)
1 teaspoon salt
½ cup chopped walnuts
grated peel of 1 orange
1 egg, beaten
1 cup milk
2 tablespoons oil or melted butter

Mix cranberries with ½ cup sugar and let stand. Sift together flour, baking powder, salt and balance of sugar. Add walnuts and orange peel and mix. Blend egg with milk and butter; stir into the nut mixture. Fold in cranberries. Pour into buttered loaf pan. Bake at 325°, about 1¼ hours, until toothpick tests clean. Turn out to cool. This will slice better the second day. If you wish to bake this ahead of time you may do so, then put it in your freezer where it will keep very well.

October

SPOTLIGHT ON BREAKFAST
GOLDEN HARVEST MONTH

Make Your Own Granola
Grain, Seed and Nut Cereal
Wholegrain Wheat Cereal
Museli
Grandma's Meal
Oven Baked French Toast and Bacon
Broiled French Toast with Cheese Filling
Honey French Toast
Ham and Egg Rolls
Basic Waffle or Pancake Mix
Wholewheat Hot Cakes
Nut Waffles
Blender Pancakes or Waffles
Soy Hot Cakes
Poached Eggs with Minced Ham on Toast
Cottage Cheese Omelet
Fortified Breakfast Eggnog
Breakfast Drink
Blender Milk Shakes
October, The Golden Harvest Month
Seasoned Salt
Hot Spiced Cider
Yam Casserole
Stuffed Yellow Squash
Spinach With Cream Cheese
Acorn Squash
Baked Eggplant
Tomato Dolma
Corn on the Cob

OCTOBER SPOTLIGHTS BREAKFAST

What is the most important meal of the day so far as your general health and well-being are concerned?

The answer is *Breakfast*. Research has demonstrated that a poor breakfast or no breakfast can sabotage your health, ruin your disposition, affect your learning capacity and deplete your energy.

To try to do a half-day's work on an almost empty stomach puts two strikes against you as far as physical fitness is concerned.

After a night without food, the body needs replenishing if it is to function effectively throughout the morning.

Sleeping as late as possible is much more important to some people than eating breakfast. We know that sleep is important, but research has demonstrated that people work better and learn more rapidly on a full stomach than on an empty one. Going without breakfast or eating a poor one also lowers body resistance and causes you to be more subject to deficiency diseases.

Studies show that you can't make up for an inadequate breakfast by eating more at lunch and dinner.

Some people say they have no time to prepare breakfast. This is not a valid excuse, for it takes less than 10 minutes to prepare an adequate morning meal of fruit, wholegrain cereal or scrambled eggs, wholegrain bread, butter and milk.

Skimping on breakfast does not cut weight as some people believe. The breakfast-skippers are often hungry by mid-morning and eat snacks before lunch or they overeat at lunch and dinner. A good breakfast can help one to lose weight if it is part of a well-planned weight reduction program.

The Mayo Clinic at Rochester, Minnesota has found that a substantial breakfast lays the foundation for a healthy life. This meal should be followed by a light lunch and a leisurely light dinner.

MAKE YOUR OWN GRANOLA

Suggested combination:

2½ cups rolled oats	½ cup soy powder
½ cup powdered milk	½ cup sesame seeds
½ cup coconut	½ cup sunflower seeds
(unsweetened)	½ cup slivered almonds
½ cup raw wheat germ	½ cup date sugar (optional)

Mix together the above. In a sauce pan put ½ cup oil, ½ cup honey and warm to mix ingredients. Place dry mixture in large shallow pan. Pour warm oil and honey over the top. Mix well. Bake at 275°, for 1 hour. Stir frequently. Cool 15 minutes, then remove to container. Serves 12-16 depending on size of servings.

GRAIN, SEED, AND NUT CEREAL

1 teaspoon sunflower seeds	1 teaspoon millet
1 teaspoon hard spring	1 teaspoon sesame seeds
wheat	1 teaspoon flaxseeds
1 teaspoon oats	4 or 5 almonds with skins
1 teaspoon rye	¼ teaspoon salt, if desired
1 teaspoon barley	

Soak the above ingredients overnight in 1 cup milk.

Next morning, cook mixture in upper part of double boiler over low heat for 10 minutes. Pour into blender with enough additional milk to enable blender to function. Blend for 30 seconds. Add 1 teaspoon bone meal and 1 teaspoon wheat germ. Blend 2 seconds. Serve with chopped dates or honey. Serves 2.

If you wish to serve this cereal as a beverage, add 1 cup unsweetened pineapple, apple or orange juice and 1 tablespoon raisins or 6 dates and juice of ½ lemon. Liquefy 3 seconds. Serves 3.

WHOLEGRAIN WHEAT CEREAL

Wash 1 cup of wholegrain wheat. In upper part of double boiler place wheat in 2 cups of milk and 1 cup of water. Have water simmering in lower part of double boiler. Place upper part over the hot water. Put on simmer burner and cook 3 or 4 hours, or until grains swell and are tender. Salt may be added to taste before serving. Serves 4. (This cereal may be cooked overnight on the pilot light of a gas range).

MUSELI

For 2 or 3 servings, soak overnight 1 cup of uncooked rolled oats in milk or water to cover. The next morning add 2 tablespoons honey, 2 teaspoons lemon juice, ¼ cup slivered almonds and some fresh fruit. Grated raw apple is often used for this dish.

GRANDMA'S MEAL

In a "Mighty Mill" or blender, grind the following to a fine meal consistency: 1 tablespoon flaxseed, 2 tablespoons sunflower seeds and 3 or 4 pecan meats. This is enough for 1 serving. I have used walnut meats or almonds instead of the pecan meat at times: they are good.

OVEN BAKED FRENCH TOAST AND BACON

2 eggs, well beaten   *Wholegrain bread, 8 slices*
1 cup milk   *Bacon, 8 strips (optional)*
½ teaspoon salt

Combine eggs with milk and salt. Dip each slice of bread in the egg mixture, place on well-greased cookie sheet. Arrange bacon strips on wire rack in shallow baking pan. Place the pan with bacon on the center rack and the bread on the rack above in the oven at 450°. Bake both until bread is lightly browned and bacon is cooked.

BROILED FRENCH TOAST, CHEESE FILLING

Between slices of wholegrain bread, place a slice of Cheddar cheese. Dip each sandwich in a batter made of 2 eggs beaten with 1 cup milk, ¼ cup dry skim milk and 2 tablespoons melted butter. Place on buttered cookie sheet under broiler and brown on both sides. Serves 6.

HONEY FRENCH TOAST

2 eggs   *Nutmeg*
2 cups milk   *6 or 8 slices of wholegrain*
¼ cup honey   *bread several days old*
½ teaspoon salt

Beat eggs until light. Warm the milk slightly and blend well with the honey. Add the salt, nutmeg and beaten eggs and mix well. Dip bread slices in mixture and lightly cook in frypan. Turn when beginning to brown. Serves 4.

HAM AND EGG ROLLS

Cook one medium chopped onion in 2 tablespoons of butter or oil until tender. Add ½ cup chopped cooked ham and 4 eggs slightly beaten. Cook, stirring frequently, until eggs are set. Salt and pepper to taste. Spread between buttered whole wheat buns, with plenty of lettuce added. Serves 4.

BASIC WAFFLE OR PANCAKE MIX

1¼ cups wholewheat flour (pastry)

3 teaspoons baking powder (tartrate)

½ teaspoon salt

2 eggs

1 cup milk (plus enough more to make a mixture that will pour)

2 tablespoons salad oil (not olive oil)

2 tablespoons honey

¼ cup wheat germ (optional)

Sift flour with baking powder and salt. Beat eggs and combine with milk, oil and honey. Stir in dry ingredients and wheat germ. Do not over-stir, just enough to mix all the ingredients.

Brush griddle lightly with oil, then heat. Drop batter by spoonfuls to make cakes of desired size. Allow to cook until cakes are bubbly on top, then flip over with pancake turner and finish cooking. Serves 4.

For variety, stir one of the following into the batter before baking:

Crumbled crisp bacon
Ground cooked ham
Shredded cheese
¼ cup finely chopped sunflower seeds
½ cup chopped dates
½ cup chopped pecans

WHOLEWHEAT HOT CAKES

1½ cups wholewheat pastry or bread flour	½ teaspoon salt
¼ cup wheat germ (optional)	1 egg
	1¼ cups sweet milk
3 teaspoons baking powder (tartrate)	2 tablespoons salad oil
	2 tablespoons honey
	1 teaspoon molasses

Sift flour, measure, sift again with baking powder and salt. Beat egg in large bowl; add milk, oil, honey and molasses. Stir in sifted dry ingredients and wheat germ. Makes a thick pour-batter. Fry lightly in a little oil until bubbles appear on one side. Turn and finish cooking.

You may make these substitutions:

½ cup soy flour for ½ cup wholewheat
¼ cup peanut flour for ¼ cup wholewheat
1 cup buttermilk or sour milk with ½ teaspoon soda for
   sweet milk

Bake pancakes, and as they come from the griddle, top each with a slice of boiled ham or 2 browned link sausages. Roll pancakes over to enclose meat. Arrange pancakes overlapping edges down in a single layer in a large pan. Brush with melted butter. Keep hot in a slow oven 250°. Serve on warm plates. Cottage cheese may be used instead of ham or other meat. Serves 4.

NUT WAFFLES

1½ cups wholewheat pastry flour	2 tablespoons honey
¾ teaspoon salt, or to taste	1¼ cups milk
2 teaspoons baking powder (tartrate)	5 tablespoons salad oil
2 eggs, separated	⅓ cup chopped walnuts or pecans

24

Sift flour, salt and baking powder. Separate eggs, beat yolks until light and combine with honey, milk and oil. Sift in flour mixture. Add chopped nuts. Beat egg whites stiff but not dry. Fold into batter, stirring no more than necessary. Bake in preheated waffle iron until crisp and brown. Serves 3 or 4.

BLENDER PANCAKES OR WAFFLES

PANCAKES:
4 eggs
1 cup milk
½ cup oil

Blend and pour over

1½ cups unsifted wholewheat flour
1 tablespoon baking powder (tartrate)

Mix well and bake. Serves 3 or 4. These make firmer pancakes than the basic recipe.

WAFFLES:

Use the blender pancakes recipe, but separate the eggs, beating the egg whites very stiff in a larger bowl and pouring the dough over them, folding it in carefully by hand. Bake in preheated waffle iron until brown. Serves 3 or 4.

SOY HOT CAKES

¾ cup soy flour
¼ cup wholewheat pastry flour
¼ teaspoon salt
½ teaspoon soda or 1 yeast cake
⅓ cup powdered milk

¾ cup sour milk (scant measure)
2 tablespoons honey
2 tablespoons melted butter or oil
3 large eggs (beaten)

Measure and sift dry ingredients. Mix together sour milk, honey and butter. Combine mixtures and stir well. Fold in beaten eggs. Do not beat mixture. Drop large spoonfuls on greased griddle and cook until bubbles appear. Turn and cook other side. Makes 20 generous cakes.

POACHED EGGS WITH MINCED HAM ON TOAST

4 slices buttered whole
 grain toast
4 poached eggs
1 cup cheese sauce

½ cup minced ham (chop leftover ham fine and mix with a little mayonnaise or sour cream)

Spread toast with minced ham. Arrange on a hot platter and top each piece with a poached egg. Pour cheese sauce over each and garnish with paprika and chopped parsley.

COTTAGE CHEESE OMELET

4 eggs, separated
½ teaspoon salt
⅛ teaspoon pepper
¼ cup milk
¾ cup cottage cheese
1 tablespoon butter

3 tablespoons finely chopped fresh green pepper or canned pimiento
2 tablespoons chopped parsley

Beat egg yolks until thick; add salt, pepper, milk, cheese and pimiento or pepper.

Fold in stiffly beaten egg whites. Place butter in skillet, melt and add omelet. Cook slowly over low fire until firm and browned on bottom. Bake in preheated, moderate oven, for 10 to 15 minutes, or until browned on top. Crease, fold, slip onto hot platter and garnish with parsley. Serves 6.

FORTIFIED BREAKFAST EGG-NOG

1 or 2 glasses of milk (certified raw if available)
1, 2 or 3 eggs
1 or 2 tablespoons powdered whole milk (if weight is a problem, use powdered skim milk)
1 tablespoon wheat germ (raw or powdered preferable but because of taste some prefer it toasted)

1 tablespoon brewer's yeast
Flavoring: choice of carob syrup, date crystals, honey, black strap molasses, banana, malt, peanut butter, vanilla, nutmeg or cinnamon and a dash of salt

Suggested mixing method: beat eggs with electric mixer, hand whipper or food liquifier; add powdered milk, wheat germ, yeast, salt and blend: add milk and flavoring and blend.

This is best served cold. Make it taste good by using small amounts or eliminating altogether any of the ingredients which are unacceptable at first.

This egg-nog could be your entire breakfast with the addition of some whole fruit. Serves 2 or 3.

BREAKFAST DRINK

Put in blender: 1 cup apple juice

Add:
1 tablespoon bone powder
2 tablespoons calcium powder
2 tablespoons whey or powdered milk or both
2 tablespoons lecithin

Add:
½ cup yeast liver mix
1 cup yogurt
¼ cup cold-pressed oil
2 tablespoons frozen orange juice
(vary amount and type of juice to taste)

Egg yolks or eggs may be added if desired. Divide evenly into 4 glasses. Dilute with milk as desired.

BLENDER MILK SHAKES

Place ¼ cup sunflower seeds (shelled), 6 almonds and 2 tablespoons toasted sesame seeds in blender or food chopper. Blend until fine. Combine the seeds and nuts with ½ cup powdered whey and 1 cup milk (certified raw if possible). Add 1 teaspoon honey and 1 teaspoon vanilla. Blend and serve.

This recipe lends itself to many additions, according to your family's preference. Some of these may be: orange juice, tomato juice, carrot juice, pulp of apricot, pineapple, papaya, mashed berries, brewer's yeast, powdered skim milk, lecithin granules, raw eggs, salad oil or molasses.

Be very careful not to mix up too many different ingredients or the taste could be so terrible the family will not drink it. Serves 2 or 3, depending on size of glass.

OCTOBER, THE GOLDEN HARVEST MONTH

Autumn brings a glorious assortment of foods, the harvest of man's efforts with nature's help: corn, pumpkin, squash, crisp new apples, pears, grapes, plums and persimmons, to name only a few.

The big orange-colored pumpkins are almost too pretty to cut for jack-o'-lanterns—but you need not throw them away when the fun is over. When the holidays come, you will be glad you took time to cook the Halloween jack-o'-lantern. From each pound of pumpkin it is possible to get about a half-cup of puree. A small, 4 to 6 pounder should yield enough for a pie or pudding; any left over can be frozen.

SEASONED SALT

6 tablespoons salt, prefer-
    ably sea salt
½ teaspoon dried thyme
    leaves
¼ teaspoon garlic powder
2¼ teaspoons paprika
½ teaspoon marjoram

½ teaspoon curry powder
1 teaspoon dry mustard
¼ teaspoon onion powder
⅛ teaspoon dill seed
several dried celery leaves
1 tablespoon dried parsley

Put all ingredients in blender and let run for a few minutes. Store in a glass jar.

HOT SPICED CIDER

For two quarts:
Peel of 1 lemon
36 whole cloves
3 inches of stick cinnamon

¼ teaspoon salt
¼ cup honey
2 quarts fresh, pure cider

Tie spices and lemon peel in a piece of cheese cloth. Combine cider, salt and honey in a sauce pan. Place over low heat, stir until honey is dissolved. Add spice bag. Bring mixture to a boil and simmer 10 minutes. Remove spice bag and keep warm while serving. Serves 6-8.

YAM CASSEROLE

4 medium-sized yams or
    sweet potatoes (about 4
    cups sliced)
2 tablespoons butter
½ cup finely chopped onion

¼ cup dry whole wheat
    bread crumbs
¼ cup grated Cheddar
    cheese
2 well-beaten eggs
1 cup sour cream

Cook yams in boiling salted water until tender. Drain, peel, cool and cut in thin slices. Melt butter, add onions and cook until tender. Put yams in a 1-quart casserole. Sprinkle on onions, bread crumbs and cheese.

Combine eggs, sour cream, salt to taste and a dash of pepper. Pour mixture over the yams. Sprinkle a little cinnamon over the top. Bake at 350°, 15 to 20 minutes. Serves 6.

I do not believe vegetables should be highly seasoned. They are delicious cooked only until tender steamed, quick-cooked in oil or baked lightly.

A little butter or herbs may be added with a dash of seasoned salt.

STUFFED YELLOW SQUASH

6 small yellow straight-necked squash

1 cup fine soft wholewheat bread crumbs

1 cup finely chopped cooked ham or cooked chicken

¼ teaspoon nutmeg

½ teaspoon salt

⅛ teaspoon ground black pepper

8 tablespoons melted butter

Wash squash, split in half lengthwise and remove seeds. Combine bread crumbs, ham, nutmeg, salt, pepper and half the butter. Spoon into cavities of the squash halves. Put halves together, tie with a string to keep in stuffing. Brown lightly in remaining butter. Reduce heat, cover and cook 20 minutes or until squash is tender, turning to cook both sides. Serves 6.

SPINACH WITH CREAM CHEESE

Cook 1 package frozen chopped spinach or 2 bunches fresh, cut up. Do not cook in too much water. There should be no liquid left. Stir into the spinach 1 3-ounce package of cream cheese and 1 minced clove of garlic or whole clove. Remove whole garlic before serving. Heat and stir to melt cheese. Serves 3.

ACORN SQUASH

3 *small acorn squashes*   1 *teaspoon salt*
¼ *cup orange juice*   2 *tablespoons butter*
¼ *cup honey*   ⅛ *teaspoon nutmeg*

Cut squashes in half. Remove seeds. Place squashes in a shallow baking pan. Combine orange juice, honey and salt. Mix well. Put some of the orange-honey mixture into each squash cavity. Add 1 teaspoon butter to each squash half. Sprinkle with nutmeg, if desired. Cover pan tightly to keep the steam in and speed cooking. Bake at 400°, 30 minutes. Remove cover and continue baking 30 minutes more or until squash is tender. Serves 4-6.

BAKED EGGPLANT

1 *large eggplant*   3 *eggs*
onion, size of walnut, diced   ½ *cup fine bread crumbs*
  fine   ¼ *cup butter*

Peel and cut eggplant into small pieces. Boil until tender in well-salted water, then drain thoroughly. Fry onion in butter until light brown. Mash eggplant, add onion and butter, bread crumbs and eggs, well-beaten. Season with salt and pepper. Turn into baking dish. Cover top of mixture with dry bread crumbs to absorb excess butter. Bake ½ hour, in 350° oven.

Grated cheese may be sprinkled over the top before placing into oven. Serves 4-6.

TOMATO DOLMA

Stuffed vegetables—or dolmas—are indigenous to Greece and other Mideast nations. The stuffing contains rice and often lamb. Seasonings include mint, dill and cumin. Pine nuts are usually used. Vegetables which can be stuffed besides tomatoes are sweet green or red peppers, zucchini, grape leaves and eggplants.

Stuffing:

2 large onions, chopped	*1 tablespoon minced mint*
½ cup oil	*or dill*
¾ cup brown rice	*Salt, pepper*
1½ pounds ground lamb or	*⅛ teaspoon cumin*
beef	*¼ cup pine nuts*

Cook onions in oil until tender but not browned. Add rice, cook and stir until golden. Remove from heat and combine with meat and mint. Salt and pepper to taste, then add cumin and nuts. Mix well. Will fill 8 to 10 tomatoes.

Cut a slice from the stem end of each tomato and scoop out pulp. Mix pulp with stuffing and pile into tomato cups. Mix ½ cup tomato sauce into 1½ cups water and pour over tomatoes. Cover and bake at 350°, for 40 minutes, adding water if necessary.

CORN ON THE COB

When buying corn, look for fresh husks with a good green color, silk ends that are free of decay and stem ends that are not discolored or dried. Avoid ears with yellowed, wilted or dried husks. Select ears well covered with pulp, not-too-mature kernels with depressed areas on the outer surface. Refrigerate until ready to use.

To boil, clean and place in boiling water or steam for 3 to 5 minutes. Do not allow to stand in hot water after cooking.

November

THANKSGIVING—THE TRADITIONAL FEAST

Stuffings—Amounts and Kinds
  Brown Rice
  Rice Almond
  Apple Nut
  Corn Bread
Timetable for Roasting at 325°
Turkey Gravy
Quick Turkey Pie
Turkey Curry
Chicken Breasts With Grapes
Pumpkin Chiffon Dessert
No-Bake Cheese Cake
Steamed Carrot Pudding—Orange Sauce
Honey Plum Pudding
Honey Rice Meringue
Blueberry Cobbler
Apple Snow
Thanksgiving Accessories
  Zagek Armenian Dip
  Stuffed Mushroom Snacks
  Chive Dill Dip
  Fruited Dip For Snack Tray
  Party Cheese Balls
  Sesame Crackers
  Cranberry Relish
  Raw Apple Relish
  Stuffed Celery
  Crab Avocado Cocktail

THANKSGIVING—THE TRADITIONAL FEAST

Roast turkey is most commonly served, but roast chicken or capon is delicious also.

If the turkey that you are serving is frozen, defrost it completely before cooking. You may use one of the following methods:

If time permits—Place on tray in refrigerator two to four days, or about 24 hours for each six pounds of turkey.

Faster—Place on tray at room temperature 1 hour per pound of turkey.

Hurry—Cover with cold water, changing water frequently.

Cook neck and giblets in water to cover for gravy or to season dressing.

A golden-roasted turkey is a rare treat, and the secret of its goodness is in the type of roasting pan used, as well as the method of roasting—(covered or uncovered)—and oven temperature. Covered roasting is really steaming the bird and the appearance is not as attractive as open roasting.

In covered roasting, a dark enamel pan can do the job an hour faster than a bright, shiny roaster. In open roasting, the turkey, stuffed and trussed, is placed on a rack over a shallow pan. Cover the turkey for the first three or four hours with an oiled or buttered piece of clean white sheeting. Remove this for the last hour of cooking, unless the turkey has become quite brown.

A meat thermometer inserted in the turkey's thigh muscle is the best method of testing doneness. When the thermometer registers 185°, remove the bird from

POULTRY WEIGHT (ready to cook) STUFFING INGREDIENTS	4 LBS.	6 LBS.	10 LBS.	12 LBS.	20 LBS.
Butter	¼ cup	⅓ cup	½ cup	⅔ cup	1 cup
Chopped Celery	½ cup	⅔ cup	1 cup	1⅓ cups	2 cups
Chopped Onion	½ cup	⅔ cup	1 cup	1⅓ cups	2 cups
Chopped Parsley	2 tablespoons	¼ cup	⅓ cup	½ cup	1 cup
Soft whole wheat bread cubes about ½" square	6 cups	9 cups	15 cups	1⅓ gallons	2 gallons
Number of slices	6	9	15	18	30
Salt and pepper to taste					
Poultry Seasoning	1⅓ teaspoons	2 teaspoons	1 tablespoon	1¼ tablespoons	2 tablespoons
Water	⅓ cup	⅔ cup	1 cup	1⅓ cups	2 cups
Approximate number of cups of stuffing	4	6	10	12	20

Note: 8 cups soft bread crumbs equal a one-pound loaf. Extra stuffing may be baked in oiled pan with turkey.

the oven and allow to rest for 20 minutes. A foil tent will keep the turkey warm during this time. Foil need not touch the bird.

BROWN RICE STUFFING

For a change of flavor in preparing stuffing for roast fowl, use cooked brown rice mixed with any of the following: cooked chopped mushrooms; toasted sesame seeds; pignolia (pine)nuts; soy grits; flaked almonds or pecans; celery and chopped parsley.

Instead of sweet potatoes, serve baked acorn squash. It is a good source of Vitamin A.

RICE-ALMOND STUFFING

Melt ¾ cup butter or use oil, add ½ cup minced onion, 1 cup diced celery and cook until tender. Add:

4 cups cooked brown rice
   (1¼ cups raw)
¾ cup slivered almonds
½ cup chopped parsley

⅛ teaspoon each ground
   sage and thyme leaves
Salt and pepper to taste

Toss lightly, stuff neck and cavity. This is enough for a 12 to 14 pound turkey. Stuff just before roasting.

APPLE-NUT STUFFING

6 cups dry wholegrain
   bread crumbs
1 cup chopped celery
1 cup chopped walnuts, or
   other nuts
1 medium onion, finely
   chopped

½ cup finely minced parsley
1 teaspoon salt
½ teaspoon pepper
2 teaspoons each sage and
   marjoram

Mix the above and put in a covered container in refrigerator overnight. The next morning add:

5 apples, peeled and diced
½ cup (1 cube) butter
  melted, or oil

1 cup water or broth from
  cooking giblets

Mix well and stuff turkey, then begin roasting at once.

CORN BREAD STUFFING

½ cup (1 cube) butter
1 cup chopped celery
¼ cup chopped onion
3 cups wholewheat crumbs,
  herb-seasoned (sage,
  oregano, parsley, onions)
  or

1 teaspoon poultry seasoning
3 cups corn bread crumbs
1¼ cups liquid from cook-
  ing giblets or chicken
  broth (1½ teaspoons
  chicken broth concentrate
  in hot water can be used)

In a 1-quart sauce pan, melt butter, add celery and onion and cook until almost tender. In a large bowl, combine corn bread crumbs, wholewheat bread crumbs and poultry seasoning. Toss together lightly, add butter mixture and turkey liquid being careful not to mash. The day you are going to roast the turkey, stuff the turkey, not the night before.

TIMETABLE FOR ROASTING AT 325°

Ready-to-Cook Weight	Time
6 to 8 lbs.	3 to 3½ hours
8 to 12 lbs.	3½ to 4½ hours
12 to 16 lbs.	4½ to 5½ hours
16 to 20 lbs.	5½ to 6½ hours
20 to 24 lbs.	6½ to 7 hours

TURKEY GRAVY

Pour off all fat possible from the liquid under the roast. You can add ice cubes to make fat particles congeal, then they can be spooned out. Often a paper towel may be lightly held to the surface of the drippings to absorb the fat.

Mix 2 tablespoons flour with ½ cup cold water. Add some of the hot meat drippings, then pour this mixture into the pan with the remaining juices, stirring constantly until gravy thickens. The drippings have a good meat flavor.

QUICK TURKEY PIE

½ cup thick cranberry sauce (preferably the kind you make yourself, using dark brown sugar)
1½ cans cream of chicken soup or turkey gravy or a combination of both
¾ cup milk
1½ cups diced leftover turkey
Cornbread topping (your favorite cornbread recipe: see January.)

Combine 3 cups of gravy and milk slowly to make a smooth sauce. Add turkey and mix well. Pour turkey mixture into buttered casserole or 8 inch square cake pan. Carefully fold cranberry sauce into cornbread batter. Spread or drop this topping over turkey mixture. Bake at 425°, 15-20 minutes. This is wonderful cooked in an electric frypan. Just drop the batter by spoonfuls onto the bubbly hot turkey mixture in frypan. Place lid on with vent closed. Cook at 300°, for 12-15 minutes without raising lid. Serves 4-6.

TURKEY CURRY

2 cups cream of celery soup
 (you can make your own)
1½ teaspoons curry powder
½ cup milk

¼ cup minced onion
½ cup sliced Brazil nuts
3 cups diced turkey
1 teaspoon lemon juice

Combine cream of celery soup, milk, curry powder, minced onion and sliced Brazil nuts. Place over low heat, stirring occasionally, until mixture comes to a boil. Add turkey and lemon juice. Heat and serve with cooked brown rice, cooked wholewheat or cooked barley. Serves 6.

CHICKEN BREASTS WITH GRAPES

4 chicken breasts, boned
¼ pound wild rice, cooked
 (can use long grain brown
 rice)
Salt, pepper and garlic salt
 to taste
4 teaspoons butter
¼ cup chopped onion
2 cups tomato puree

½ cup chopped mushrooms
1 tablespoon chopped
 parsley
1 teaspoon chicken broth
 concentrate
1 tablespoon grated orange
 rind
1 cup fresh seeded or seedless grapes

Stuff chicken breasts with rice, seasoned with salt and pepper. Shape meat around rice. Fasten with a toothpick if necessary. Dot each breast with butter. Place in a casserole and bake in a preheated 400° oven until brown.

Saute onions, add tomato puree, mushrooms, parsley, chicken broth concentrate, orange rind and seasonings. Simmer 15 minutes. Add grapes and simmer 5 more minutes. Pour over cooked breasts of chicken. Simmer 10 minutes more. Serves 4.

PUMPKIN CHIFFON DESSERT

2 envelopes unflavored
    gelatin
1 cup brown sugar, packed
1 teaspoon cinnamon
½ teaspoon nutmeg
¼ teaspoon salt

½ teaspoon ginger
¾ cup milk
1¾ cups pumpkin (mashed)
3 eggs, separated
½ cup whipping cream or
    honey-sweetened yogurt

Combine gelatin, brown sugar, salt and spices in top of double boiler. Add milk, pumpkin and slightly beaten egg yolks, mixing well; cook and stir over hot water about 10 minutes until slightly thickened. Chill until mixture starts to thicken. Beat egg whites stiff, fold into pumpkin mixture. Whip cream and fold in or, if yogurt is used, fold it in. Pour into an oiled mold and chill until firm. Unmold on serving plate. Garnish with additional whipped cream or yogurt. Serves 4-6.

NO-BAKE CHEESE CAKE

2 envelopes plain gelatin
¼ teaspoon salt
¾ cup honey
1 cup milk
3 eggs, separated
1 teaspoon vanilla

1 teaspoon grated lemon
    peel
2 tablespoons lemon juice
3 cups cottage cheese
1 cup whipping cream
bread crumbs

In sauce pan, mix gelatin with salt and honey. Stir in milk and egg yolks, mixing well. Cook over low heat, stirring constantly, until mixture comes just to boiling and is slightly thickened. Remove from heat; add vanilla, lemon juice and peel. Press cottage cheese through strainer or beat in an electric blender until fairly smooth. Stir hot mixture into this. Chill until it will mound slightly when dropped from spoon. Beat egg whites almost stiff; beat cream stiff and fold both into the thickened gelatin. Pour into crumb-lined 9 or 10-inch spring form pan; sprinkle top with crumbs. Crumbs can be finely rolled wholewheat bread crumbs. Chill until firm. Serves 12.

STEAMED CARROT PUDDING

1¼ cups unbleached white flour or pastry flour
1 teaspoon baking powder (tartrate)
½ teaspoon salt
1 teaspoon pumpkin pie spice
½ cup butter or oil
½ cup brown sugar or honey
1 egg, beaten
1 tablespoon water
½ cup chopped nuts
1 cup grated raw carrots
2 teaspoons grated orange peel
½ cup chopped dates

Sift together flour, baking powder, salt and spice. Cream butter with sugar. Add egg, water, nuts, carrots and orange peel. Dust dates with ¼ cup flour mixture, then stir into butter mixture. Beat in remaining flour. Turn into greased covered 1½-quart pudding mold. Steam 1 hour. Serve with orange sauce. Serves 4-6.

ORANGE SAUCE

3 tablespoons cornstarch
½ cup honey
¼ teaspoon salt
¼ cup shredded orange peel
2 cups orange juice
1 cup water

In heavy saucepan, combine cornstarch, honey and salt. Stir in orange peel, orange juice and water; cook over low heat, stirring constantly until thickened. Cool and serve on pudding.

HONEY PLUM PUDDING

½ cup butter, softened
1 cup honey
1 egg, beaten
⅔ cup buttermilk
2½ cups sifted wholewheat
    flour
1 teaspoon soda
1 teaspoon each baking
    powder and cinnamon

½ teaspoon cloves
¾ teaspoon salt
rind of 1 orange, grated
½ cup raisins
½ cup chopped dates
½ cup other dried or
    candied fruit
honey butter sauce

Mix butter and honey. Add egg and buttermilk. Then add dry ingredients and mix well. Fold in rind and fruit. Spoon batter into greased 2 quart mold. Put on rack in kettle of boiling water, allowing water to come halfway up around the mold. Cover and steam about 3 hours. Serve hot with sauce.

HONEY BUTTER SAUCE: Mix together ½ cup soft butter, ¼ cup honey and 1 teaspoon cinnamon. Stir until well blended.

HONEY RICE MERINGUE

2 cups milk
3 tablespoons unbleached
    white flour
3 eggs, separated
1½ cups cooked brown rice

5 tablespoons honey
2 tablespoons melted butter
1 teaspoon vanilla
1 teaspoon lemon juice

Make a soft custard of the milk, flour and egg yolks. Fold in the rice, 2 tablespoons of the honey, butter and vanilla. Pour into oiled baking dish. Bake at 350°, about 20 minutes. Remove and cover with meringue made of beaten egg whites, 3 tablespoons of the honey and the lemon juice. Warm the honey so that it is thin when you mix it with the whites. Pile on the pudding, return to 400° oven for a few minutes. Serves 4-6.

BLUEBERRY COBBLER

1½ cups + 1 tablespoon
   sifted wholewheat flour
2 teaspoons baking powder
½ teaspoon salt
3 tablespoons butter

⅓ cup + 2 tablespoons
   brown sugar
1 egg well beaten
¾ cup milk

Sift dry ingredients several times. Cream butter and 2 tablespoons of the sugar, add egg and milk. Stir in flour mixture, stirring only enough to mix.

Place 2 cups or 1 package frozen blueberries in a 1½-quart baking pan.

Mix ⅓ cup brown sugar with 1 tablespoon flour and sprinkle over berries and mix well.

Spread dough over sweetened fruit. Bake for 30 minutes at 350°. Serve while hot. Serves 4.

APPLE SNOW

Shred two medium size unpeeled, unsprayed apples with a fine shredder. Add 1 teaspoon lemon juice, 1 tablespoon honey and ⅓ cup chopped raisins or dates. Blend well. Serve in sherbet glasses and sprinkle with grated coconut. Serves 2-3.

THANKSGIVING DINNER ACCESSORIES
ZAGEK ARMENIAN DIP

1 bunch spinach
½ cup parsley minced
1 tablespoon dried mint

4 cloves garlic
4 cups yogurt
Salt to taste

Chop spinach and cook 2 minutes. Drain. Add

44

chopped parsley, mint, garlic, yogurt and salt. Serve as a dip. Serves 10-15.

STUFFED MUSHROOM SNACKS

Mix 1 cup yogurt with 3 tablespoons finely chopped green onion and 2 tablespoons minced parsley; let stand in refrigerator 12 hours.

Wash and gently pull out stems of fresh mushrooms. Marinate caps in mixture of ½ apple cider vinegar and ½ oil for 3 hours in refrigerator. Drain. Fill caps with yogurt mixture. Serve as hors d'oeuvres or with entree.

Variation: Omit marinade. Fill caps and serve raw or place in 350° oven, covered for 10 minutes or until hot. 1 pound fresh mushrooms serves 10-15.

CHIVE DILL DIP

8 ounces cottage cheese	Dash celery salt
2 tablespoons chopped chives	¼ teaspoon dill seed
	Few drops hot pepper sauce

Combine cheese, chives, celery salt, dill and pepper sauce. Beat until fluffy or process in a blender until light. Makes 1 cup.

FRUITED DIP FOR SNACK TRAY

If your snack assortment seems too tangy flavored, add this fruited dip to the tray.

Soften an 8 ounce package of cream cheese at room temperature and blend in 1 cup chopped walnuts and ½ cup chopped dates. Fold in 1 cup chopped apple and serve with assorted crackers. Serves 6-10.

PARTY CHEESE BALLS

These can be made ahead and frozen.

½ cup grated Swiss cheese
½ cup grated jack cheese
1 package (8 ounces) cream cheese
1 wedge (3 ounces) bleu cheese, shredded
½ pound sharp Cheddar cheese, shredded
¼ cup minced onion

Dash of Worcestershire sauce
1 tablespoon sherry wine (optional)
⅔ cup finely chopped walnuts
⅓ cup finely chopped parsley

Bring cheese to room temperature. Mix with onion, Worcestershire sauce and wine and form into one, two or three balls. Roll each in combined nuts and parsley. Wrap in refrigerator paper and refrigerate or freeze. Bring to room temperature to serve. Serve with wholewheat crackers. Serves 10-15

SESAME CRACKERS

2 cups buttermilk
1 teaspoon soda
½ cup oil
¼ cup toasted sesame seeds
Enough wholewheat pastry flour to make a soft dough

Blend buttermilk, soda, oil and sesame seeds with enough flour to make a soft dough. Roll thin and cut into strips or circles with a biscuit cutter. Bake on greased cookie sheet in a slow oven at 325°, for 15-20 minutes. If crackers become soft, heat in hot oven for a few minutes. The number that you make depends on how you cut them. Can make about three dozen.

CRANBERRY RELISH

Put through grinder 2 cups raw cranberries and 1 medium orange, seeded. Combine ground cranberries and orange with ½ cup walnuts cut up and enough honey to sweeten to taste. Do not add too much: the relish should be tart and also thick. Chill. Serves 8-10.

RAW APPLE RELISH

2 large apples, peeled and cored
¼ cup cauliflower, raw, cleaned and washed
1 carrot, raw
¼ medium onion
¼ green pepper
2 tablespoons lemon juice
¼ teaspoon powdered ginger
Salt and pepper to taste

Chop the apples, cauliflower, carrot, onion and pepper very, very fine. Blend these. Add all other ingredients and mix well. Serve with meats as an appetizer. Makes 2 cupfuls.

STUFFED CELERY

Blend 2 3-ounce packages cream cheese with 1 tablespoon milk, 2 tablespoons finely chopped nuts, ⅓ cup finely chopped dried figs and ⅛ teaspoon ginger. Stuff celery. Makes about 1 cup.

CRAB AVOCADO COCKTAIL

1 cup cooked or canned crab
¼ cup mayonnaise
1 tablespoon lemon juice
1 tablespoon prepared horseradish
1 tablespoon chili sauce
1 avocado

Remove any bits of shell or cartilage from crab meat. Blend mayonnaise, lemon juice, horseradish and chili sauce. Add to crab meat and toss to blend. Cut avocado in half, then in quarters, removing pit and skin. Place each quarter avocado on greens. Spoon crab mixture into avocado. Serve at once. Serves 4.

December

GIFTS FROM THE KITCHEN

Cookies
  Pumpkin Date Cookies
  Persimmon Cookies
  Carrot Cookies
  Honey Walnut Cookies
  Carob Potato Cookies
  Honey Peanut Butter Cookies
  Honey Butter Fingers
  No-Bake Peanut Butter Treats
Cake
  Applesauce Fruit Cake
  No-Bake Fruit Cake
  Orange Honey Fruit Loaf
  Honey Spice Cake
  Carrot Cake
  Raw Apple Cake
Sweets
  High Protein Vitamin Candy
  Sesame Butter Candy
  Candied Citrus Peel
  Stuffed Apricots
  Baked Caramel Corn
  Sesame Fruit Balls
  Peanut Butter Slices
  Dried Fruit Lollipops

GIFTS FROM THE KITCHEN

Ever since the three kings brought their gifts of gold, frankincense and myrrh to the Holy Child nearly two thousand years ago, the giving of gifts has had a special meaning.

The gifts you make at this Christmas season are more symbolic of the true meaning of Christmas than that of any other kind.

PUMPKIN DATE COOKIES

¾ cup shortening (butter) or oil
2 cups brown or raw sugar
2 eggs, beaten
1½ cups cooked pumpkin
1 teaspoon vanilla
1 cup chopped dates and nuts
¼ cup dry skim milk powder
2¼ cups wholewheat pastry flour
3 teaspoons baking powder (tartrate)
½ teaspoon each: salt, nutmeg, cinnamon
¼ teaspoon ginger

Cream shortening and sugar. Add remaining ingredients. Mix well. Drop by teaspoonfuls on a greased cookie sheet. Bake at 350°, for 15 minutes. Makes 5 dozen.

PERSIMMON COOKIES

½ cup butter
1 cup brown sugar
1 egg
2 cups unbleached flour
½ teaspoon cinnamon
½ teaspoon nutmeg
1 cup persimmon pulp without seeds or skin
½ teaspoon soda
1 teaspoon baking powder (tartrate)
1 cup chopped nuts
1 cup chopped raisins
1 cup chopped dates

Cream butter and sugar together. Add egg. Add sifted dry ingredients alternately with persimmon pulp, soda and baking powder. Then add nuts, raisins and dates. Drop by teaspoonfuls on greased cookie sheet. Bake at 350°, for about 10 to 12 minutes. Makes 5 dozen.

CARROT COOKIES

1 cup butter	4 tablespoons dark brown sugar
½ teaspoon salt	
1 teaspoon vanilla	2 cups pastry wholewheat flour, sifted
1 cup chopped nuts	
1 cup grated carrots	2 teaspoons baking powder (tartrate)

Cream butter, add salt, vanilla, nuts and carrots. Combine sugar, flour and baking powder and stir into first mixture. Mix well. Form mixture into 2 rolls. 1-inch in diameter. Wrap in waxed paper and chill 2 hours. Slice ½-inch thick and bake on ungreased cookie sheet at 375° for 10 to 12 minutes. Makes 6 dozen.

HONEY WALNUT COOKIES

½ cup butter	½ teaspoon soda (soda will be neutralized)
⅓ cup honey	
2 eggs	¼ teaspoon salt
1 teaspoon grated lemon peel	½ teaspoon nutmeg
	½ teaspoon cinnamon
1¼ cups pastry wholewheat flour	½ cup coarsely chopped walnuts
½ teaspoon baking powder	

Cream butter while adding honey in a fine stream. Blend in eggs and lemon peel. Sift flour with dry ingredients; add to creamed mixture. Stir in chopped walnuts.

Honey dough is very soft. To make cookies hold their shape, you must chill the dough for 1 hour or longer. Drop by teaspoonfuls on greased cookie sheet, about 2 inches apart. If desired, lightly press a walnut half into top of each cookie. Bake at 325° (moderate), 10 to 12 minutes, or until lightly browned. Do not overbake. Keep remaining dough refrigerated between bakings. Makes about 3 dozen.

CAROB POTATO COOKIES

1½ cups unbleached flour	1 teaspoon vanilla
½ teaspoon salt	1 egg, beaten
½ teaspoon soda	¼ cup carob powder
½ cup butter	½ cup cold mashed potatoes
1 cup brown sugar	½ cup chopped nuts

Sift flour, salt and soda. Cream butter and sugar, stir in vanilla and egg and combine with flour mixture. Add carob powder, potato and nuts. Mix well. Drop by teaspoonfuls on oiled cookie sheet. Bake at 400° about 10 minutes. Makes 3 dozen.

HONEY PEANUT BUTTER COOKIES

2 cups honey	1½ cups rolled oats
1½ cups chunk-style peanut butter	2 cups raisins, chopped
3 unbeaten eggs	1½ cups sifted wholewheat flour
1 tablespoon water	1 teaspoon salt
1 teaspoon vanilla	1 teaspoon soda

In a large mixing bowl combine honey, peanut butter, eggs, water and vanilla. Blend well. Stir in oats, raisins and flour sifted with salt and soda. Drop by teaspoonfuls on oiled cookie sheet. Bake at 350°, for 8 to 10 minutes. Do not overbake. Cookies continue baking after removal from the oven until removed from cookie sheet or until the sheet cools. Makes 5 dozen.

HONEY BUTTER FINGERS

Spread wholegrain bread slices with honey butter. Sprinkle with sesame seeds. Cut bread in finger-length strips. Toast in hot oven 8 to 10 minutes or until crisp and golden.

To make honey butter, blend ½ cup butter with ½ cup honey. Beat thoroughly. Store in refrigerator.

NO-BAKE PEANUT BUTTER TREATS

2½ cups oats (put in blend-
    er while dry, to break
    them until quite fine)
½ cup non-homogenized
    crunchy peanut butter
1 teaspoon vanilla
¼ cup milk

1¾ cups cream honey if you
    have it; liquid honey
    will do
⅛ teaspoon salt
6 tablespoons carob
    powder

Combine oatmeal with peanut butter and vanilla in a bowl. Mix the milk, honey, salt and carob powder in a pan, bring to a boil, allowing mixture to boil for 1 minute. Pour this hot mix over the rolled oats, peanut butter and vanilla. Mix lightly until blended. Drop from a teaspoon onto lightly oiled paper or cookie sheet. Let stand until firm. Makes about 3 dozen cookies.

APPLESAUCE FRUIT CAKE

1½ cups thick applesauce, unsweetened
1 cup brown sugar
½ cup butter (one cube)
⅓ cup molasses
2 tablespoons vinegar
2 eggs, slightly beaten
2 cups unbleached flour
3 teaspoons baking powder
1 teaspoon salt
2 teaspoons cinnamon
½ teaspoon each cloves, nutmeg, allspice
1 cup walnuts, chopped
1 cup dates, sliced
1 cup prunes, sliced
¾ cup seedless raisins
1 cup dried apricots, sliced
¼ cup citron, sliced
½ cup wholewheat pastry flour

Heat applesauce with sugar and butter; cool. Stir in molasses, vinegar and eggs. Sift 2 cups of flour with baking powder, salt, cinnamon, cloves, nutmeg, allspice. Stir into applesauce mixture. Mix nuts and fruits with ½ cup of flour and stir into batter. Spoon into 2 oiled and brown-paper lined small bread pans or 1 large bread pan. Bake at 300°, for about 2½ hours for small pans and 3 hours for 1 large pan.

NO-BAKE FRUIT CAKE

½ cup butter
½ cup honey
1 teaspoon cinnamon
¼ teaspoon nutmeg
½ teaspoon salt
1 teaspoon vanilla
2 tablespoons lemon juice
20 graham crackers, crumbled

½ cup of each:
Seedless raisins
Dates, pitted and cut up
Figs, cut in slivers
Apricots softened ½ hour in little water, then cut up
Citron, cut in slivers
Orange peel, cut in slivers
Almonds, slivered
Walnuts, chopped

Cream butter and honey; add spices, salt and flavorings. Pour over cut fruits and nuts, mix and let stand 2 hours. Add cracker crumbs, mix well and pack into 9x13 inch glass dish or other pan. Cover, store in a cool place. Will keep refrigerated several months.

ORANGE HONEY FRUIT LOAF

2 cups sifted unbleached
  flour
½ teaspoon salt
4 teaspoons baking powder
  (tartrate)
2 tablespoons grated
  orange peel
1 medium orange, peeled,
  cut up, drained

⅔ cup honey
½ cup chopped raisins
½ cup coarsely chopped
  nuts
1 egg, beaten
½ cup water
3 tablespoons melted
  butter

Sift flour, salt and baking powder together. Combine orange peel, cut-up fruit, honey, raisins, nuts, egg, water and butter in a bowl. Add dry ingredients, stirring only enough to mix well. Pour into well-oiled 9x5x3 inch loaf pan. Bake at 350°, for 1 hour. Insert a toothpick to test for doneness—it should come out clean.

Remove from pan onto rack.

HONEY SPICE CAKE

½ cup shortening
1 teaspoon vanilla extract
1 cup honey
2 eggs
¼ cup sifted pastry wholewheat flour
½ teaspoon salt

1½ teaspoons baking
  powder
¼ teaspoon baking soda
¼ teaspoon nutmeg
½ teaspoon cinnamon
1¾ cups fine graham cracker crumbs (22 crackers)
⅔ cup milk

Cream shortening and vanilla. Add honey in fine stream while creaming. Continue creaming until light and fluffy. Add eggs one at a time, beating well after each addition. Sift together flour, salt, baking powder, baking soda, nutmeg and cinnamon. Mix lightly with graham cracker crumbs. Add alternately with milk to creamed mixture. Start and end with dry ingredients. Pour into well-greased cake pan (8x12 inch). Bake at 350°, (moderate) 35 to 40 minutes.

Topping: Unusual and delicious ... equal amounts of honey, peanut butter and nonfat dried milk.

CARROT CAKE

1½ cups dark brown sugar	1 teaspoon baking soda
1½ cups salad oil (not olive)	1 teaspoon salt
4 eggs unbeaten	2 teaspoons cinnamon
2 cups sifted unbleached flour	1 teaspoon mace
3 teaspoons baking powder	3 cups grated raw carrots
	1 cup chopped walnuts

Mix oil and sugar thoroughly. Add eggs and beat well. Sift flour, baking powder, soda, salt and cinnamon. Add to oil mixture. Fold in grated carrots and nuts. Bake in greased 10x13 inch pan at 325°, for 1 hour. Frost when cool with 8-ounce package of cream cheese to which has been added ¼ cup spray-dried powdered milk and enough honey to make it spreadable. Be careful not to add too much honey or it will be sticky.

RAW APPLE CAKE

1 cup oil
2 eggs
2 cups dark brown sugar or 1½ cups honey
2 teaspoons soda
1 teaspoon salt
2 cups sifted pastry wholewheat flour
4 cups apples, peeled and chopped fine

Mix all the ingredients together, and pour into a greased pan, 13x9 inches. Bake at 350°, for 60 minutes. Serve with whipped cream. Serves 12-16.

HI-PROTEIN VITAMIN CANDY

1 mixing bowl
⅓ cup safflower oil or soya
⅓ cup honey
1 tablespoon rice polish

2 tablespoons carob powder
1 teaspoon brewer's yeast
1 teaspoon vanilla
Skim milk powder

Mix oil and honey well, add rest of ingredients, and then keep adding skim milk powder until it is thick enough to roll out like a pecan roll. Nuts, raisins or sunflower seeds may be added in mixing. Spread onto oiled waxed paper and refrigerate. When cold cut into slices.

SESAME BUTTER CANDY

Combine the following, roll and slice:

½ cup tahini (sesame butter)
¾ cup carob powder
⅓ cup honey

½ cup coconut (dried, not sugared)
½ cup sunflower seeds
1 tablespoon molasses

This candy always tastes better the next day. Store in the refrigerator. You can always add more liquids or more dry ingredients until you get the consistency *you* like.

CANDIED CITRUS PEEL

Candied peel should be made from undyed, unwaxed and preferably organic fruits. Use the peel of 3 large oranges, 2 medium grapefruits, or 6 average size lemons. Cut all fruit away from peel. Cover with water to which has been added 1 teaspoon salt. Simmer for 30 minutes. Drain and cover with water and simmer until tender. Drain again; cut into narrow strips. Put back into pan and cover with 2 tablespoons of boiling water mixed with enough honey to just cover peel. Simmer very slowly until peel is clear (about 45 minutes). Lay on waxed paper and let stand 2 or 3 days before using. Roll in fine coconut, chopped nuts, or coat with carob powder.

STUFFED APRICOTS

Soften dried apricots in a 300° oven for a few minutes, or steam until just limp. Roll the apricot around a nut meat, then roll it in ground nuts or powdered dry milk.

BAKED CARAMEL CORN

½ cup butter
⅓ cup dark brown sugar
3 quarts unsalted popped corn

1 cup whole pecans or mixed nuts (optional)

Cream butter and brown sugar until fluffy. Combine popcorn and nuts with sugar/butter mixture. Place on buttered cookie sheet. Bake at 350°, about 8 minutes, or until crisp.

SESAME FRUIT BALLS

½ pound pitted dates
⅓ cup seedless raisins
½ pound dried apricots
2 tablespoons honey

2 ounces sesame seeds
or
½ cup coconut, grated

Put the fruit through meat grinder. Add the honey

and mix thoroughly. Roll into small balls between the palms of the hands. Roll the balls in lightly toasted sesame seeds or coconut. Makes about 2 dozen.

PEANUT BUTTER SLICES

A good substitute for candy

½ cup peanut butter (not homogenized)
½ cup honey

Powdered milk (spray dried, not instant) from health food store

Combine the peanut butter and honey. Stir in enough powdered milk to make the mixture like soft dough. You may need to work this with your hands until it is blended. Shape into long rolls about 1½-inches in diameter. Place in refrigerator to harden, then cut into slices.

DRIED FRUIT LOLLIPOPS

6 pitted dried prunes
8 dried apricot halves

4 plump dried figs

Pour boiling water over dried prunes. Let stand for 5 minutes. Drain; when cool enough to handle, roll prune between thumb and forefinger to loosen pit. Slit each prune just enough to remove pit.

Pour boiling water over apricots and figs; let stand for 3 to 5 minutes, drain. Thread 3 pitted prunes, 4 apricots and 2 figs alternately on small wooden skewers or lollipop sticks. Makes 2 lollipops.

(Note) The fruit may be steamed soft instead of placed in boiling water. Seedless raisins can be plumped by washing and spreading them out in a flat pan. Cover. Heat slowly in moderate oven at 350° until they puff up and the wrinkles come out.

January

SOUPS AND CASSEROLES

Basic Soup Stock
Beef Vegetable Soup
Scotch Broth
Pepper-Pot Soup
Potassium Broth
Tomato Soup Without Milk
Tomato Soup
Popcorn Italian
Scallop Stew
Maine Clam Chowder
Parsley Soup
Lentil Soup
Lentil Carrot Soup
Senate Restaurant Bean Soup
Dumpling Bits
Soybean Casserole
Spinach Meat Dinner Dish
Ala-Tuna Casserole
Fruit Soup

SOUPS AND CASSEROLES

Who says soup must be confined to noonday or evening meals? In our modern way of life, with its informal meals, that simply isn't so.

On a cold winter morning, nothing hits the spot like a bowl of hot soup before heading out for work or school, and it presents a marvelous departure from regular breakfast fare.

I've tried this out on my students and have had a grateful response—they're glad to have something so nourishing and easy to prepare for breakfast.

While there are some good canned and frozen soups on the market, you will probably find you'll prefer the ones you make yourself. They can be frozen and heated up for any time of the day.

Serving soup in cups and mugs is also part of the appeal to youngsters—and cuts down on dishes for the housekeeper, too. At more formal meals, it can be ladled from a tureen, served from a chafing dish or poured from an attractive jug or pitcher.

And instead of crackers, serve it with a warm loaf of homemade bread, topped with onion pieces, sesame or poppy seeds. Good, fragrant, wholewheat bread can whet many a lagging appetite when served with hot, tantalizing soup. Soup can be the main dish for any meal.

A potful of fragrant hot soup keeping warm on the back of the stove, ready to serve to a happy, hungry family on a cold winter's night, is symbolic of all that we treasure most: the united family gathered round one common board.

A soup rich with vegetables and meat becomes a

full meal when combined with a hot bread, a salad and fruit, such as pears or tart apples, for dessert.

In the heart of the winter, one dish meals are somehow more satisfying than more conventional menus. Perhaps Time is the reason—arrivals are uncertain in bad weather and we want something reliable and on hand for dinner. At any rate, the casserole recipes here are enjoyed with the same simple accompaniments as the hearty main dish soups.

BASIC SOUP STOCK

1 *knuckle bone, cracked*
2 *tablespoons vinegar*
1 *teaspoon salt*
1 *medium onion, cut in pieces*

3 *garlic buds, cut in half*
1 *cup mixed vegetables and their leaves*

Brown bone in large pan. Add remaining ingredients and cover with water to top of pan. Simmer 8 to 10 hours. Refrigerate overnight. Peel off hardened fat. Heat and flavor in any of the following ways: seasoned salt, bouquet garni, your favorite herbs to taste. Add to the hot soup cooked vegetables of your choice or grated raw carrots, grated raw beets, chopped parsley, leftover ground beef or chicken, uncooked bean sprouts, sliced fresh onions, parmesan cheese or mashed avocado. Serves 6 or 8.

BEEF VEGETABLE SOUP

1 *beef shank or several marrow bones*
1 *tablespoon salt*
1 *cup diced carrots*
1 *cup chopped celery leaves and stems*
2 *peeled tomatoes or 1 can tomatoes*

⅓ *cup barley*
1 *medium chopped onion*
½ *cup finely chopped parsley*
1 *bay leaf*
1 *pinch thyme*
1 *pinch basil*
5 *cups cold water*

Brown bone in oiled skillet and transfer to soup kettle. Cover meat and bones with water. Bring to a boil and skim until surface is clear. Add remaining ingredients, and when soup boils again add barley very slowly. Cover and simmer 3½ hours, adding more water as needed. For vegetable stew, add more vegetables in the amounts you like, cut as you please and cook until barely tender. Serves 4-6.

SCOTCH BROTH

½ cup split peas
½ cup Bulgar wheat or
    barley
2½ cups light vegetable
    stock or water
1 carrot, chopped

½ cup chopped celery
1 small leek, chopped
1 teaspoon parsley
2 teaspoons grated carrots
Salt and pepper to taste

Add split peas and Bulgar to boiling stock. Simmer gently for 1 hour. Add all ingredients except grated carrot. Cook over medium heat until broth is thick. Stir occasionally and if mixture is too thick, add more broth or water. Add the grated carrot and dumpling bits if desired.

Variation: add ⅓ pound of raw cubed beef or lamb, with peas and wheat. Serves 6-8.

PEPPER-POT SOUP

6 tablespoons chicken broth
    concentrate in 6 cups
    boiling water
1 bay leaf
1 teaspoon salt
1 teaspoon pepper
⅛ teaspoon thyme
½ pound honeycomb tripe,
    cut in small pieces

2 cups cubed potatoes
4 slices bacon
1 cup chopped onion
1 cup chopped green
    peppers
2 stalks celery, chopped
2 tablespoons flour
½ cup cream (optional)

To boiling soup stock add: bay leaf, salt, pepper, thyme and tripe. Simmer for 2-3 hours. Add potatoes. Cook bacon in skillet. Break into small pieces but do not remove from skillet. Add onion, green pepper and celery. Cook slowly until onions are transparent. Stir in 2 tablespoons flour, and slowly add ½ cup broth from soup kettle. Stir until thickened, and add to soup. Simmer 30 minutes or until flavors are blended. Stir in cream just before serving. Serves 6-8.

POTASSIUM BROTH

Simmer together for 20 minutes:
5 carrots, sliced thin   *1 quart of water*
1 bunch of celery, cut thin
1 bunch parsley, cut fine

Five minutes before cooking time is up, add ½ pound spinach, cut up.

Now you have a choice: strain out the vegetables and season with butter and serve the broth as a soup; or serve the pot of vegetables as a soup seasoned to taste. Serves 4.

TOMATO SOUP WITHOUT MILK

Chop three stalks of celery with leaves, 1 medium onion and 6 large ripe tomatoes. Put in saucepan with 1 cup chicken broth (may be made with concentrate), 1 small bay leaf and 3 sprigs parsley. Cook gently, covered, until celery is tender. Put through blender and reheat with vegetable salt to taste and a dash of cayenne. Serves 4.

TOMATO SOUP

6 ripe tomatoes	Pinch of oregano
1 tablespoon grated onion	1 basil leaf
1 cup water	1 cup milk
3 tablespoons soy oil	Salt and pepper to taste

Liquefy the tomatoes in blender. Add everything but milk and refrigerate overnight. The next morning, warm tomato mixture; stir in milk. Do not cook. Serves 4.

POPCORN ITALIAN

Serve with tomato soup:

Melt 4 tablespoons butter in a small skillet. Add 1 small clove of crushed garlic and 3 tablespoons grated Cheddar or parmesan cheese. Then toss in 1½ or 2 cups of popped popcorn.

SCALLOP STEW

1 medium onion, chopped	1 quart of milk
2 tablespoons butter	Salt
1 pint bay scallops or	Pepper
sea scallops cut in half	Paprika
	Chopped parsley

(For a special stew, oysters and cream may be included—1 pint cream or milk and 1 pint oysters)

Saute onion in butter until transparent. Add scallops (and oysters if included) for 1 minute, until hot (and the oysters curl). Combine with very hot but not boiling milk and keep just under the boil for 4 or 5 minutes. Season, sprinkle with chopped parsley and serve. Serves 4-6.

MAINE CLAM CHOWDER

1 quart clams or 2 large
    cans
¼ pound salt pork
1 quart diced potatoes

1 onion, chopped
1 quart of milk heated
Salt and pepper to taste

Remove black parts from clams, saving the liquor. Cut pork in small pieces, fry until golden crisp and brown, then remove them from the fat and discard the fat. Add potatoes and onion with just enough water to be seen through the potatoes. Cook at simmering until done. Add clams and cook 2 minutes. Remove chowder from heat and allow to stand a few minutes, then add hot milk, the clam liquor and seasonings to taste. Serves 6. This tastes even better the next day.

PARSLEY SOUP

3 tablespoons olive oil
1 medium onion, chopped
½ small can tomato sauce or
    2 medium tomatoes
Salt to taste

1 bunch washed, chopped
    parsley
5 cups water
3 or 4 garlic buds, chopped
1 cup whole wheat or soy
    spaghetti, cooked

Lightly cook onion in the olive oil a few minutes. Add tomato sauce, parsley and water. Cook 5 minutes, then add garlic and spaghetti. Cook together 5 minutes. Salt to taste and serve.

LENTIL SOUP

A bowl of robust bean soup takes the chill out of a wintry day. These long-simmered soups give a cozy warmth to the kitchen also.

    Lentil soup is brimming with a blend of appetizing

flavors. Dried beans may be substituted for lentils and chicken, turkey or ham stock substituted for beef.

1½ cups dried lentils	1 cup diced carrots
6 cups cold water	2 whole cloves
1 cup chopped onion	2 bay leaves
½ clove garlic	2¼ teaspoons salt
4 cups beef stock	Dash of pepper
2 cups chopped celery	3-4 tablespoons vinegar

Cover lentils generously with water and soak them overnight. Measure remaining water, adding enough to make 6 cups. Add all other ingredients and cover; simmer until lentils are soft. Add vinegar and, if needed, more salt and pepper. Serves 8 to 12.

LENTIL-CARROT SOUP

1 cup lentils	½ teaspoon basil
1 tablespoon butter	1 tablespoon parsley, chopped
2 tablespoons onion, chopped	1 cup carrots, diced
3 quarts soup stock (use concentrate if necessary)	1 cup lettuce, shredded
½ teaspoon marjoram	Salt, cayenne
	Lemon

Soak lentils in 2 cups of water overnight. Melt butter in sauce pan; add onions and brown. Add soup stock and herbs. Add lentils and cook slowly for 1 hour. Then add the carrots and lettuce and cook ½ hour longer. Rub through food mill or sieve, reheat, and add salt to taste and a dash of cayenne. Shave a washed lemon in very thin slices, put in a tureen and pour the hot soup over. Serve at once.

SENATE RESTAURANT BEAN SOUP

1½ pounds pea or navy
   beans
4 large yellow onions,
   chopped
1 large clove garlic
6 sprigs parsley

¾ teaspoon thyme
1½ large bay leaves
1 carrot, chopped
½ lemon
1 pound ham hock or shank
   end of smoked ham

Put beans in large bowl, cover with 4 or 5 inches of water and soak overnight. Next day drain, put in large soup kettle and cover with 3 quarts of water. Brown onions and garlic in a little butter and add to pot. Make a bouquet garni of herbs, carrot and lemon, tie in cheesecloth, and drop in kettle. Add ham. Cover and cook slowly for about 3 hours or until the beans are done. Remove garni and discard. Remove ham and cool; take out 2 cups of beans with liquid, puree, and return with 2 cups of water. Cut ham in small pieces and return to soup. Season with salt and freshly ground pepper. Reheat carefully. Freezes well. Serves 8.

DUMPLING BITS

3 tablespoons wholewheat
   flour
1 egg

½ teaspoon parsley
Salt to taste

Mix in order given. Drop by small bits into boiling soup. Reduce heat, cover at once and simmer for 10 minutes. Serves 6 to 8.

CORN BREAD TO SERVE WITH SOUP
OR CASSEROLE

Sift 1½ cups yellow stone ground corn meal, 2 tablespoons wholewheat flour and 1 teaspoon salt into a bowl. Stir in 2 tablespoons oil and 2 tablespoons honey. Fill a measuring cup with boiling water (1 cup). Pour in a very slow stream over the corn meal. Stir while pouring.

Beat the whites of 3 eggs and add the yolks to the beaten whites, one at a time. Beat after each addition. Fold into the corn meal mixture, being careful not to break down whites. Pour into 8-inch oiled pan. Bake at 450°, 5 minutes; then reduce heat to 350° until bread is brown and a tester comes out clean. Serves 4-6.

SOYBEAN CASSEROLE

Add 1 cup dry soybeans to 3 cups boiling water and soak overnight. Drain and rinse. Add the following:

Small ham hock or 1 tablespoon oil	*2 peeled, chopped tomatoes or 1 can tomatoes*
1 small diced onion	*2 bay leaves*
¼ cup diced celery	*2 teaspoons salt*
1 clove crushed garlic	*⅓ cup unsulphured molasses*

Add water to cover. Bring to a boil, lower heat and simmer for 2½ hours. Molasses may be omitted. Serves 6 or 8.

SPINACH MEAT DINNER DISH

½ pound ground beef	*Salt and pepper to taste*
1 chopped medium onion	*1 package chopped frozen spinach*
1 chopped garlic bud	*2 eggs*
½ cup sliced celery	*sour cream*
¼ teaspoon oregano	

Sauté the first six ingredients until meat is cooked. Cook frozen spinach for a few minutes. There should be no liquid to drain. Add spinach to meat mixture. Stir in 2 eggs, one at a time. Cook until eggs are set. Serve with sour cream. Serves 4.

ALA-TUNA CASSEROLE

1 cup ala (bulgar wheat, can be obtained in grocery stores)
  may substitute cooked brown rice
2 tablespoons butter
2 cups water
½ teaspoon salt

1 7-ounce can tuna
1 10½ ounce can mushroom soup
2 tablespoons chopped green onion
¼ cup buttered wholewheat bread crumbs

Sauté ala in butter until golden. Add water and salt; cover. Bring to a boil. Reduce heat; simmer 15 minutes. Carefully combine flaked tuna with mushroom soup, green onion, seasonings (such as more salt, dash of pepper and cayenne), cooked ala. Place in greased 1 quart casserole and top with buttered crumbs. Bake at 350° for 20 minutes. Serves 4 to 6.

FRUIT SOUP

1 cup unsweetened orange juice
1 cup unsweetened pineapple juice
Juice of 1 lemon
½ cup water

2 teaspoons cornstarch or 4 teaspoons arrowroot powder
3 tablespoons cold water
Honey to sweeten
Pinch of cinnamon
Sliced strawberries or peaches or blueberries or a combination (optional)

Place juices and ½ cup water in saucepan. When hot, add cornstarch mixed smooth with cold water. Add

72

fruit, if desired, and cook slowly, stirring constantly until clear. Add honey to taste. Serve ice cold as a dessert, in frosted glass sherbet dishes. Other fruit juices may be used, singly or mixed. Serves 2 or 3. A good dessert after a casserole dinner.

February

FISH—AN IMPORTANT FOOD—WITH COMPANION DISHES

Broiled Fish
Stuffed Whole Fish
Shrimp Cocktail and Cocktail Sauce
Fish Fondue
Salmon Croquettes
Fish Fillets with Herbs
Shrimp Coconut Curry
Pink Rice
String Beans with Olive Oil
String Beans with Celery and Onions
French Peas
Mushrooms with Almonds
Lemon Parsley Potatoes
Seasonings for Spinach
Festive Carrots
Carrot Pennies
Nutritious Hash Dessert
Orange-Prune-Walnut Whip
Vanilla Rice Custard
Raw Applesauce
Uncooked Milk Gelatin
Raw Prunes
Molded Orange Dessert
Uncooked "Chocolate" Pudding

FISH—AN IMPORTANT FOOD

When buying fresh fish, look for fresh mild odor; bright, clear, convex eyes; red gills; firm, springy flesh; bright and tight scales.

Fresh fish keeps best when stored in the upper section of the refrigerator or in a meat keeper. Place the dry, dressed fish in a covered dish or wrap it loosely in transparent plastic. Flavor will be best if the fish is cooked within 24 hours.

For frozen fish and shellfish the best storage temperature is zero degrees. They should be kept frozen solid in the original wrapping until you are ready to prepare them.

Never refreeze raw fish. Do not defrost frozen fish or shellfish at room temperature. Partially thaw them in the refrigerator or under cold water. Shellfish may be cooked without defrosting.

Fish is marketed in four main forms: dressed, whole fish, drawn fish and fillets and steaks.

Select fish that is refrigerated or displayed on crushed ice.

Bake or broil fish such as barracuda, herring, mackerel, salmon, shad, snapper, tuna, pompano. Poach or steam lean fish such as cod, flounder, halibut, sea bass and most white fleshed fish.

The easiest and least messy way of preparing fish is to bake it. Fish properly baked doesn't have the strong odor associated with fish cooked in other ways. Baking provides opportunity to cook fillets, steaks and whole fish with less odor in the kitchen. Clean-up is easier if the fish is cooked on a rack, over a foil-lined pan.

If you are puzzled as to how much fish to buy for your family, it is a good idea to plan on ⅓ of a pound of boned fish fillets or steaks for each person. Allow about ½ pound (bone in) of whole fish for each serving.

Fish is a good food, as it is a prime source of good protein, supplies trace minerals, vitamin D, and the fat is high in polyunsaturated factors. Fish is low in calories for the high quality nutrients it provides.

A menu consisting of baked or broiled fish with any of the vegetable dishes in this chapter—such as lemon parsley potatoes, French peas, and molded orange dessert to finish—can equal any meat dinner. In February particularly, we need the nutrients fish can give us after several months with less sun than is good for us. The other February recipes are included with fish in mind.

BROILED FISH

¼ cup soft butter
½ teaspoon salt
⅛ teaspoon pepper

1½ tablespoons minced herbs
Fish fillets, or split and cleaned small whole fish

Combine all ingredients except fish, working well with a fork until thoroughly mixed. Good combinations of herbs are basil, chives and parsley or dill and parsley. Spread seasoned butter on fish. Broil until fish flakes with a fork: 4 or 5 minutes for fillets, about 10 minutes for small split fish.

STUFFED WHOLE FISH

3 to 4 pounds whole fish—
whitefish, halibut, fresh-
water bass or trout
1½ cups whole wheat bread
crumbs
½ teaspoon dried chervil or
1 teaspoon fresh

1 tablespoon chopped
parsley
1 teaspoon salt
¾ cup milk
1 medium onion
½ cup melted butter or oil
½ cup whole corn meal
½ cup light cream

Clean and split fish. Mix crumbs, seasonings, milk and
grated onion with 3 tablespoons melted butter or vegetable oil. Stuff fish with mixture and close with skewers or toothpicks. Roll the fish in remaining oil, then
in corn meal. Put in greased pan. Bake 20 minutes at
350°. Add cream and bake until tender, ten or fifteen
minutes, basting with juices. Serve with lemon
wedges. Serves 6.

SHRIMP COCKTAIL

Put 1 tablespoon of cocktail sauce in the bottom of
each glass. Add 3 chilled shrimp, then another tablespoon of sauce, then fill glass to the brim with shrimp
and cover with cocktail sauce. Serve with lemon
wedges. Serves 4.

COCKTAIL SAUCE

¾ cup tomato ketchup
2-4 tablespoons fresh
grated horseradish or
¼ cup prepared horse-
radish

10 drops Tabasco sauce
1 tablespoon Worcester-
shire sauce
2 tablespoons lemon juice
¼ teaspoon salad oil

Mix ingredients and serve with fish, meat or cubed
avocados.

FISH FONDUE

Either shrimp, crab, tuna or flaked lobster may be used. To ½ cup of the fish add 1 cup finely diced celery.

Butter thin slices of wholewheat bread. Alternate layers of fish and bread in a 1½-quart greased casserole.

Combine 3 beaten eggs, 2¾ cups milk, 2 teaspoons Worcestershire sauce and dash of Tabasco. Pour over mixture. Bake 45 minutes in a 350° oven. Serves 4.

SALMON CROQUETTES

1¾ cups cooked salmon
(1 large can or 2 small)
2 tablespoons oil or butter
⅓ cup unbleached flour
1 cup milk
Salt and pepper to taste

1 teaspoon lemon juice
1 beaten egg mixed with 1
tsp. water
1 cup wholewheat toasted
crumbs

Make a white sauce by melting butter, stirring in the flour and slowly adding the milk. Stir until thickened. Add salt and pepper to taste. Stir in flaked, cooked salmon and lemon juice. Cool.

Shape into 6 rolls, roll in bread crumbs, egg and crumbs again.

Brown in a small amount of oil, turning croquettes frequently. Serve with tartar sauce. Serves 4-6.

FISH FILLETS WITH HERBS

¼ cup chopped onion
¼ cup chopped green
pepper
2 tablespoons chopped
parsley

2 tablespoons lemon juice
½ teaspoon dry mustard
½ teaspoon basil leaves
1 pint sour cream
Fish fillets, broiled

Blend ingredients carefully. Spoon sour cream mixture over hot broiled fish fillets and sprinkle with paprika. Return to broiler for 2 or 3 minutes to glaze sauce. Serves 4-6.

SHRIMP COCONUT CURRY

2 cups milk
1 cup flaked coconut
1½ cups deveined, cooked
   shrimp
½ cup butter
1 teaspoon curry powder
⅓ cup chopped green onion
⅓ cup chopped celery

½ cup unbleached flour
¼ teaspoon garlic salt
1¼ cups chicken broth (you
   can use 1¼ teaspoons
   chicken concentrate to
   make broth)
   hot cooked brown rice

Combine milk and coconut. Simmer, stirring occasionally, over low heat about 2 minutes until mixture foams. Cool slightly. Strain, pressing out as much of the creamy coconut pulp as possible. Reserve the coconut. Sauté shrimp in ¼ cup butter for a few minutes. Remove from skillet. Add remaining butter to skillet; stir in curry until smooth and cook over low heat 2 minutes. Add onion and celery; cook until soft but not browned. Blend in flour and salt. Slowly stir in chicken broth and the coconut flavored milk. Cook and stir until thickened. Simmer a few minutes. Stir in shrimp and half the coconut. Heat until hot through. Serve over hot cooked natural brown rice. Sprinkle with remaining coconut. Serves 4.

Serve in small sea shells or bowls: peanuts, raisins, chutney, pineapple and coconut chips to accompany this curry.

PINK RICE

1 cup brown rice
3 tablespoons butter
1 small onion grated
1 cup tomato juice

1¼ cups beef broth (can be
    made with concentrate)
Minced parsley

Sauté rice in butter in large heavy frying pan, stirring often. Stir in onion, tomato juice and bouillon; cover tightly. Cook over a low fire, 40 to 50 minutes, stirring once. Rice will absorb all of the liquid and be dry and tender. Serve with minced parsley as a garnish. Serves 4.

STRING BEANS WITH OLIVE OIL

½ cup olive oil
4 onions chopped
2 pounds fresh or
2 packages frozen string
    beans

1 cup tomato juice
1 teaspoon salt
½ teaspoon pepper

Heat oil in a sauce pan. Add onions and cook over low heat for 10 to 15 minutes, stirring frequently. Do not brown onions. Add the beans; cover and cook over low heat for 10 minutes, stirring occasionally. Add the tomato juice, salt and pepper, cooking 5 minutes longer over low heat. Serves 8.

STRING BEANS WITH CELERY AND ONIONS

1 pound fresh or
1 package frozen string
    beans
2 tablespoons butter

¼ cup chopped celery
2 tablespoons chopped
    onion
Salt and pepper to taste

Cook string beans with celery and onion, covered, in very small amount of water. Add butter as desired, when cooked. Note: do not over-cook. There should be no water remaining on the vegetables. Serves 4.

FRENCH PEAS

2 cups fresh or frozen peas   ¼ cup butter
½ head lettuce   ½ teaspoon salt
1 onion

Shred lettuce, cut onion in thin slices. Put peas, onions and lettuce in sauce pan, add butter and seasonings. Cook over medium heat, stirring frequently until peas are tender. Serves 4.

MUSHROOMS WITH ALMONDS

Try creamed mushrooms with almonds for a meatless party dish. Sliver ¼ cup blanched almonds. Place in shallow pan with ½ teaspoon butter or oil. Roast in slow oven 300° for 20 to 25 minutes until lightly browned. Stir frequently. Slice 1½ cups of fresh mushrooms (or 1 cup canned) and cook slowly in 1 tablespoon butter about 5 minutes. Stir into 1 cup medium thick white sauce. Add almonds, serve at once in bread baskets.

To make bread baskets: Cut crusts off 6 slices wholegrain bread. Butter and press buttered side down in muffin wells to make a cup. Toast until brown in 400° oven. Remove and fill with mushroom mixture. Serves 4.

LEMON PARSLEY POTATOES

Brush or scrape 12 small new or red potatoes. Cook them in small amount of water until tender. Drain and shake over heat to dry. Add 2 tablespoons of melted butter and 5 tablespoons of lemon juice. Shake and turn potatoes gently so all pieces will be flavored. Sprinkle with chopped parsley. Serves 3.

SEASONINGS FOR SPINACH

Cook spinach leaves only in water that clings to their leaves after washing. Season with any of the following: undiluted mushroom soup, about ½ cup; butter; bacon pieces; vinegar; lemon juice; chopped hard-boiled eggs; herbs such as fresh oregano or rosemary; sesame seeds; sour cream or yogurt.

FESTIVE CARROTS

1 bunch (1 pound) carrots
2 tablespoons oil (or ¼ cup boiling water)
½ teaspoon salt
¼ cup butter
¼ cup honey
2 teaspoons grated orange rind
¼ cup slivered toasted almonds

Scrub carrots and pare, if necessary. Slice diagonally into very thin pieces. In a 10-inch skillet cook the carrots in 2 tablespoons oil until tender-crisp, about 5 minutes. (Carrots may be cooked in boiling water 5 minutes). Push carrots to one side of skillet. Add butter, honey and orange rind to other side and mix over low heat. Combine with carrots and sprinkle with almonds. Serves 4.

CARROT PENNIES SEASONED WITH CUMIN AND SOUR CREAM

Scrub and slice carrots in thin rounds. Steam until tender. Season with a little sour cream, salt and dash of cumin powder. Four large carrots serves 4.

NUTRITIOUS HASH DESSERT

Mix 1 cup yogurt with ¼ cup uncooked rolled oats and 6 tablespoons honey. Blend and refrigerate overnight. An hour before serving, mix in 1 cup raw diced apple, 1 tablespoon lemon juice, ¼ cup orange juice, ½ cup cashew nuts and ½ cup whipped cream. Serves 4.

ORANGE-PRUNE-WALNUT WHIP

1 envelope unflavored
    gelatin
⅓ cup honey
½ cup cold water
1 cup fresh orange juice
3 tablespoons fresh lemon
    juice

1 cup chopped, cooked
    prunes
½ cup chopped walnuts
1 cup orange chunks,
    drained

Mix gelatin, honey and water in top of double boiler. Heat over hot water until gelatin and honey dissolve, stirring constantly. Remove from heat; cool, then stir in orange and lemon juice.

Chill until mixture is slightly thicker than the consistency of unbeaten egg white. Beat with rotary or electric beater until mixture is light and fluffy and double in bulk. Fold in chopped prunes, walnuts and orange chunks. Pour into 1-quart mold; chill until firm. Serves 6.

VANILLA RICE CUSTARD

3 tablespoons cooked
    brown rice
1 cup milk
1 egg slightly beaten

3 tablespoons dark brown
    sugar
1 teaspoon vanilla
½ cup raisins

Mix all ingredients. Pour into two custard cups; grate

fresh nutmeg over the top. Set cups in pan of hot water. Bake at 325° for about 1 hour or until almost set to the center. It will finish thickening after being removed from the oven and you will be sure of its not getting overdone. Serves 2.

RAW APPLESAUCE

Mix cut-up apples in blender until smooth. Add a little lemon or orange juice to prevent discoloration. Sweeten with honey if necessary. Four medium size apples serves four.

(Do not use seeds, but do use skins if organically grown, in making raw applesauce. Seeds have a cyanide factor.)

UNCOOKED MILK GELATIN

1 tablespoon or 1 envelope unflavored gelatin
¼ cup water
2 eggs
3 tablespoons honey
1 tablespoon vanilla
salt
2 cups milk

Dissolve gelatin in water over double boiler. Beat eggs until creamy; add honey, vanilla and dash of salt. Stir in milk and gelatin mixture. Pour into molds and serve with sliced bananas or orange slices. Serves 4.

RAW PRUNES

Soak prunes—3 for each person to be served. Pit and blend pulp with honey and lemon juice. Serve over vanilla yogurt.

MOLDED ORANGE DESSERT

1 cup yogurt
¼ cup lemon juice
¼ teaspoon salt
1 can (8 ounce) pineapple
  tidbits
1 tablespoon unflavored
  gelatin

1 package (10 ounce)
  frozen strawberries
  thawed
1 cup fresh orange sections,
  drained

Combine yogurt with lemon juice and salt. Blend well. Drain pineapple. Soften gelatin in pineapple juice and heat until dissolved. Stir into yogurt. Add berries. Beat with rotary beater.

Chill until mixture begins to thicken. Stir in pineapple and orange sections. Pour into 1-quart mold and chill until set. Unmold on lettuce, if used as a salad or serve in sherbet glasses. Serves 6.

UNCOOKED "CHOCOLATE" PUDDING

(Without chocolate or cocoa)

1 or 2 cups juice, or water
  or soya milk
2 medium large apples, cut
  up
2 medium large carrots, cut
  fine
2 dozen naturally dried,
  pitted olives. (If olives
  are too dry, they may be
  soaked a bit before pits
  are removed. Be sure no
  pits go into the blender.)

1 ripe banana (optional)
½ cup sunflower or
  pumpkin seeds
¼ teaspoon cinnamon
Ginger and cloves to suit
  taste
2 or 3 tablespoons honey or
  raw sugar
Juice of ½ lemon, if desired

Place ingredients in blender, making sure not to overload it, and blend well. This gives a delicious "chocolate" flavored mixture, without cooking, thanks to the naturally ripened, slightly bitter black olives, which are not cured with chemicals. If dried olives are not available (they usually can be found at health food stores) raisins may be substituted if ⅓ cup instant carob drink powder is added. This mixture may be used as a meal in itself if enough sunflower or pumpkin seeds (½ cup or more) are included. Serves 4-6.

March

NEW WAYS FOR VEGETABLES

MEAT ENTREES

Vegetable Curry
Asparagus, Petit Peas and Mushroom Casserole
Mushroom Green Beans
Sesame Green Rice
Cheese Mushroom Casserole
Sauce for Asparagus
Rice and Bean Sprouts
Celery Almond Casserole
Pickled Beets
Dill Dressing
Mock Hollandaise for Asparagus
Raw Asparagus Salad
Rotate Meats in Freezer to Keep Freshness
Hints in Defrosting Meats
Swiss Meat Loaf
Meatless Hamburgers
Braised Sirloin Tips With Mushrooms
Porcupine Beef Balls
Stuffed Beef Balls
Grilled Hamburgers
Juicy Meat Loaf
Armenian Meat Balls
Healthburgers
Roast Beef
Yorkshire Pudding

NEW WAYS FOR VEGETABLES

Is your family slowing up on eating vegetables? Maybe it is because you are serving them in the same old way each day. At this time of year, before the fresh vegetables arrive, we get in a rut with the preparation of the vegetables that are available.

Here are some suggestions for preparing vegetables for variety.

Broiled: Place vegetables, brushed with melted butter and seasoned, on pan in broiler compartment, three inches from direct heat. Cook until tender. Broil such vegetables as raw tomatoes, peeled, sliced eggplant, raw or cooked mushrooms, raw sliced potatoes, precooked asparagus, precooked whole onions and precooked squash.

Steamed: Place prepared vegetables in perforated steamer pan over boiling water. Cover. Steam until tender. It requires a longer time to steam vegetables, but this method conserves vitamins and minerals. Steam any vegetable except tomatoes, cabbage, onions and greens. These vegetables could lose some nutrients into the water below. Especially good when steamed are lima beans, potatoes, asparagus, corn on the cob and squash. You can steam-cook without water in heavy steel pan.

Baked: In heated oven (350-420°) place prepared vegetables in baking pan. Add butter and seasonings to vegetables before baking when not covered with skin. Bake until fork tender. Bake such vegetables as potatoes, onions, beets, squash, carrots, corn in husk, stuffed or plain tomatoes, stuffed eggplant and stuffed peppers.

Stir-fry (Chinese way): Prepare vegetables in small pieces. Heat just enough butter or oil to prevent vegetables from sticking to pan. Do not heat to smoking point. Add prepared vegetables, season and stir occasionally until just tender and lightly browned.

Pan-wilted: Add clean, thinly sliced or shredded vegetables to melted butter or oil (3 tablespoons to each quart of vegetables) in heavy pan. Season and cover. Cook slowly until tender. Stir occasionally. Use this method for such vegetables as cabbage, carrots, onions, green beans, potatoes, celery, parsnips and greens.

With herbs and spices: Add herbs and spices to vary flavor of vegetables. Use sparingly to suit taste. Add caraway seeds to turnips, sauerkraut; dill to turnips, cabbage, cauliflower, string beans. Use rosemary with potatoes, turnips, cauliflower; savory with green beans or peas; mustard seeds with beets or to garnish salads. Nutmeg adds flavor to asparagus, carrots, yellow crookneck squash, spinach. Mint is good with peas and carrots; basil with beets and tomatoes. Paprika is useful as a garnish for many vegetables, especially white.

VEGETABLE CURRY

2 *cups string beans cut in small pieces*	*Vegetable oil (warmed)*
	½ *teaspoon curry powder*
1 *cup green peas, frozen or fresh*	½ *teaspoon paprika*
	1½ *teaspoons cumin seed*
1 *large potato, peeled and diced*	1 *tablespoon chopped onion*
3 *large carrots, peeled and diced*	¾ *cup yogurt*

Place vegetables in boiling water to just cover. Cook 5 minutes. Add spices and onion to warmed oil. Combine and cook over low flame until vegetables are barely tender. Add yogurt and salt and pepper to taste. Serve over hot brown rice. Serves 4.

ASPARAGUS, PETIT PEAS AND MUSHROOM CASSEROLE

Lightly cook 2 pounds of washed, cleaned asparagus. Arrange half the asparagus in a buttered 2½-quart casserole. In a bowl, mix gently 2 cups tiny green peas, 1 can cream of mushroom soup (or make your own soup) and ¾ cup grated sharp cheddar cheese. Spoon half the mixture into the casserole; add remaining asparagus, and cover with other half of mushroom mixture. Toss 1 cup wholewheat bread crumbs with 2 tablespoons melted butter and sprinkle on top of casserole. Bake in 350° oven for about 30 minutes, or until crumbs are golden. Serves 8.

MUSHROOM GREEN BEANS

1 package frozen French style green beans or 2 cups fresh cut beans
½ cup water
1 teaspoon chicken concentrate
½ pound fresh mushrooms, sliced
2 tablespoons butter

Cook green beans until just tender; drain if necessary. Sauté mushrooms in butter; stir into beans; season with salt and pepper. You can use 1 can (3 ounces) sliced mushrooms, drained, using the mushroom liquid for cooking the beans. Serves 4.

SESAME GREEN RICE

Sauté lightly in 3 tablespoons butter:
⅓ cup finely chopped celery
¼ cup finely chopped green onions
Add:

2 cups steamed brown rice   *3 tablespoons toasted*
1 teaspoon salt   *sesame seed*
¼ teaspoon crushed thyme   *¼ cup finely chopped*
                                                  parsley

Heat together and toss lightly until well mixed. Just before serving add parsley. Makes 2½ cups. Can be used as a dressing for chicken. Serves 4-6.

CHEESE MUSHROOM CASSEROLE

May be prepared hours ahead and stored in refrigerator for last minute baking. Grease a 1½-quart casserole.

Set aside to drain 1 4-ounce can sliced mushrooms, reserving liquid contents. Cut into ½-inch slices ½ pound sharp Cheddar cheese. Trim crusts from and cut into thirds 6 slices of bread. Arrange some bread fingers on bottom of casserole. Cover with layer of ½ of the cheese and mushrooms. Repeat layering, top with remaining bread fingers. Dot with 2 tablespoons butter. Add to reserved mushroom liquid milk or half-and-half to make 1 cup liquid.

Beat until thick 2 eggs. Beat in the liquid and ½ teaspoon salt, ½ teaspoon paprika, ⅛ teaspoon pepper. Pour over layers in casserole. Bake 325°, 30 to 40 minutes or until puffed and lightly browned. Serves 6.

RICE AND BEAN SPROUTS

3 tablespoons sesame seeds
2 minced green onions
1 tablespoon salad oil
1 clove garlic, minced

1½ cups bean sprouts
2 cups cooked brown rice
2 tablespoons soy sauce

Toast sesame seeds in a heavy frying pan, stirring until they are brown and puff slightly. Crush in a bowl with a wooden spoon. Combine with onion and garlic and cook in oil for 3 minutes. Carefully stir in the bean sprouts and heat. Add a few drops of water to keep the sprouts from sticking. Combine with them the brown rice and soy sauce, mix well and serve. Serves 4-6.

CELERY ALMOND CASSEROLE

3 cups sliced celery
Boiling salted water
¼ to ½ cup slivered almonds
1 tablespoon butter
1 cup drained cooked peas

Cook ½ cup celery and thicken as for soup or use ½ can celery soup
½ cup grated Cheddar cheese
½ cup buttered wholewheat bread crumbs

Cook celery in a small amount of boiling salted water until barely tender. Cook almonds in butter until lightly browned. Stir in celery soup and peas. Place half the celery in a greased 1-quart casserole. Top with half the almond mixture and half the cheese. Repeat layers and top with bread crumbs. Bake at 350°, for 20 minutes or until bubbly. Serves 6.

PICKLED BEETS

Make a syrup of ½ cup lemon juice, ½ cup honey and 1 cup water. Pour this over small cooked beets. Refrigerate 24 hours before serving.

DILL DRESSING

Spring weather seems to call for fresh, delicious salads and dressings. Dill dressing is a nice complement to fresh vegetable salads. It can be used as a dip for vegetable sticks, including crisp, tender, cooked young asparagus or raw, tender shoots. To make the dill dressing, combine 1 tablespoon vinegar, ¾ teaspoon salt, dash pepper, 2 teaspoons honey, 1 teaspoon dill weed and 1 cup sour cream. Makes 1 cup.

MOCK HOLLANDAISE FOR ASPARAGUS

4 tablespoons butter
2 tablespoons flour
¾ cup chicken broth
¼ cup sauterne (optional; can use white vinegar)
¼ teaspoon salt
Dash of pepper and cayenne
2 egg yolks
1 teaspoon lemon juice

Melt 2 teaspoons butter, blend in flour, broth and sauterne. Add salt, pepper and cayenne. Cook, stirring constantly, until mixture has boiled and is thickened. Stir slowly into lightly beaten egg yolks. Return to very low heat and cook, but do not boil, about 1 minute longer, stirring constantly, until sauce thickens slightly and egg is cooked. Remove from heat and add remaining butter and lemon juice, stirring until butter is melted. Serve at once over hot cooked asparagus. Serves 6.

SAUCE FOR ASPARAGUS

Mix thin mayonnaise with a little lemon juice and heat gently over hot water. Makes a quick, pleasant sauce for asparagus.

RAW ASPARAGUS SALAD

Raw vegetables for salads should be of good color, free of blemishes, young and tender. Asparagus should be freshly picked, deep green and should not have thick stalks. Raw, slim, tender, 1½ to 2-inch spears can be used in tossed green salad.

Marinate the raw asparagus for 2 or 3 hours in the following marinade: mix and beat with ½ cup oil, ¼ cup lemon juice or vinegar, 1 teaspoon honey, ¼ teaspoon paprika, ¼ teaspoon garlic powder, ¼ teaspoon onion powder (freshly grated onion and garlic are even better), ¼ teaspoon vegetable salt or regular salt. Enough for 2 pounds of asparagus.

ROTATE MEAT IN FREEZER
TO KEEP FRESHNESS

Freezers kept below 0° F. can keep food for a long time. However, no frozen food will maintain quality indefinitely. Storage of foods for longer than 1 year is not recommended.

It is not that the food becomes unfit to eat, it is just that it loses quality. This is why it is important that as you add meat you shift the meat that has been frozen longer closer to the freezer door so that you will use it first.

Although refreezing foods is not a recommended procedure, frozen foods can be refrozen safely as long as they are still partially frozen or are below 40°, but there is some sacrifice of quality—juiciness for example.

Here is the storage time recommended for meat held at 0° or lower.

Fresh beef 6 to 12 months; fresh veal 6 to 9 months; fresh pork 3 to 6 months; fresh lamb 6 to 9 months.

Ground beef, veal or lamb may be stored 3 to 4 months. Fresh pork sausage may be kept frozen for 60 days. Smoked ham may be kept frozen 60 days; corned beef for 2 weeks. Leftover cooked meat may be kept frozen for 2 to 3 months.

HERE ARE HINTS IN DEFROSTING MEATS

When defrosting meat before cooking, the most practical method is in your refrigerator, or at room temperature. Meat should be defrosted in its original wrapping and should be cooked immediately after thawing.

For a large roast allow 4 to 7 hours per pound in your refrigerator; 2 or 3 hours per pound at room temperature. The original temperature of the cut, the defrosting temperature and the shape of the cut (chunkier cuts require more time) are all factors that affect the time.

For a small roast allow 3 to 5 hours per pound in your refrigerator; 1 to 2 hours per pound at room temperature.

A 1-inch steak requires 12 to 14 hours in the refrigerator; 2 to 4 hours at room temperature.

SWISS MEAT LOAF

2 pounds ground beef
1½ cups diced Swiss cheese
2 beaten eggs
½ cup chopped onion
1½ teaspoons salt
½ teaspoon pepper
1 teaspoon celery salt
½ teaspoon paprika
¼ cup chopped parsley
2 cups milk
1 cup dry wholegrain bread crumbs

Mix in order given. Bake at 350° for about 1½ hours. Recipe serves 8. Leftovers may be used in sandwiches.

MEATLESS HAMBURGERS

2 cups farmer style cottage
  cheese
1 cup fine wholewheat
  bread crumbs
  (set aside ½ cup)
¾ teaspoon salt

1 tablespoon finely
  chopped green pepper
2 tablespoons finely
  chopped onion
1 egg, slightly beaten
2½ teaspoons ground
  sunflower seeds

Combine all ingredients, form into 8 cakes and cover each with reserve crumbs. Chill ½ hour. Brown on both sides in butter or oil. Serve with chili sauce.

BRAISED SIRLOIN TIPS WITH MUSHROOMS

1½ pounds sirloin tip steak,
  ¾ inch thick
Seasoned flour (salt, pepper)
3 tablespoons oil
1 medium onion, sliced

8-ounce can sliced mush-
  rooms
½ cup water or broth
¼ cup dry red wine or
  water

Coat steaks with seasoned flour. Brown slowly and thoroughly in hot oil. Add onion after turning steaks and let brown lightly, then add mushrooms and their liquid, water and wine. Cover and cook slowly on top of range or in 350° oven about 1 hour or until meat is tender. Serves 6.

PORCUPINE BEEF BALLS

Lightly grease a 2½-quart casserole having a tight-fitting cover.

Combine 1 pound of ground beef, ½ cup uncooked brown rice and ¼ cup minced onion, as well as a mixture of 1 teaspoon salt, ½ teaspoon chopped basil and a dash of cayenne pepper. Shape into 1½-inch balls and place in the casserole.

Pour 2 cups of tomato sauce over meat balls. Cover and bake at 350° about 1 hour or until the visible rice is tender when pressed lightly between the fingers. To serve, garnish with parsley. Serves 4 to 6.

STUFFED BEEF BALLS

1 egg	¼ teaspoon cumin powder
1 cup fine wholewheat bread crumbs	¼ cup minced onion
	½ cup milk
½ teaspoon salt	1 pound ground beef
¼ teaspoon oregano	Stuffings

Combine egg (slightly beaten), bread crumbs, salt, oregano, cumin powder, onion, milk and ground beef. Mix well and shape into 24 small balls or 12 larger balls. Stuff with any of the following: ½-inch cube Cheddar cheese, small pitted ripe olive; tiny button mushroom; ½-inch cube cooked potato; or ½ teaspoon chili beans, drained.

Reshape into balls, place on shallow baking pan. Bake small balls at 425°, about 10 minutes; bake larger balls at 400°, about 25 minutes. Serve the small ones as hors d'oeuvres and the larger ones with a meal. A cheese or tomato sauce should be served over the larger ones. Serves 4 to 6.

GRILLED HAMBURGERS

1 pound ground beef mixed with ½ teaspoon salt, ¼ teaspoon pepper, 1 tablespoon grated onion, ½ cup cheddar cheese cubes and ⅛ teaspoon chili powder. Divide into 8 even portions and form into patties ½-inch thick.

Pour 1 teaspoon oil on each grid or on griddle and cook patties until brown; turn and cook 5 to 7 minutes on other side.

Toast wholewheat buns, spread butter on buns and the cooked hamburger.

JUICY MEAT LOAF

1½ pounds ground beef
1 egg
1 cup tomato juice or milk
1 cup rolled oats
½ cup finely chopped onion
1 small bud garlic, chopped fine

½ cup parsley chopped fine
¼ teaspoon oregano or thyme
1½ teaspoons salt

Beat egg, then add tomato juice. Add remaining ingredients, mix well. Form into a loaf or fit into a greased loaf pan. Stick a few cloves in the top and lay a bay leaf on the top. Bake in a moderate oven, 350°, for 1 to 1½ hours. Serves 6.

ARMENIAN MEAT BALLS

(To serve with a rice dish)

Combine 2 pounds of thrice-ground beef or lamb, 2 teaspoons salt, a little pepper, 1 cup finely minced onion and 1 cup minced parsley. Form into balls about 1 inch in diameter. Brown in ½ cup butter or oil. When they are brown transfer to a dish to keep warm. To the pan add ½ cup shelled pine nuts and brown them slightly. Add 2 tablespoons tomato paste and 2½ cups water. Simmer 5 minutes and serve on meat balls. Serves 4-6.

HEALTHBURGERS

1 pound ground beef
¼ cup wheat germ
¼ cup buttermilk
1 teaspoon salt

¼ teaspoon pepper
2 tablespoons minced onion

Combine all ingredients thoroughly. Shape into 6 patties. Grill, broil or fry as desired. Serve in hamburger buns.

ROAST BEEF

Purchase boned, rolled rump, chuck or standing rib roast of 2 or 3 ribs.

The heel of round may be roasted at low heat and is delicious.

Insert meat thermometer in flesh, but not near the bone. Place on rack over drip pan. Do not cover. Roast in 325° oven until thermometer reads desired degree of doneness—140° for rare, 160° for well done. Serves 4-6.

YORKSHIRE PUDDING

½ cup wholewheat pastry
  flour (sifted)
2 eggs (beaten)

½ teaspoon salt
1 cup milk

Mix all ingredients thoroughly. In a 9-inch pie pan, place ⅛ cup of beef drippings taken from the roasting beef. Place under the roast in the oven until drippings are sizzling.

Pour Yorkshire Pudding mixture in the hot pan and bake 40 minutes.

April

EGGS RATE HIGH AS FOOD

EASTER FARE

Size Affects Recipes
Scrambled Eggs Mexican
Eggs in a Frame
Eggs Italian
French Eggs
Avocado Omelet
Spanish Potato Omelet
Eggs and Whole Grain Rice
Egg Salad Mold
Ham and Egg Casserole
Lollipop Eggs
Eggs in Toast Nests
Egg Salad for Summer Luncheon
Egg Tuna Pie
Eggs Baked in Tomato Shells
Pickled Eggs
Tuna-Egg-Soup Sandwich
Avocado with Chicken Salad
Avocado Mousse
Greek Chicken
Fruit Pie for Easter
Minted Fresh Pineapple
How To Cook With Vanilla Bean

EGGS RATE HIGH AS FOOD

The eggs so popular on Easter morning are being neglected as food according to a study of the menus of 2,450 homemakers conducted by the United States Department of Agriculture. It was found that the use of eggs as breakfast, lunch and dinner food had been declining. Four reasons were given for this.

1. Most adults now consider eggs to be a food for breakfast only and two out of five don't even eat eggs for breakfast.

2. Eggs are considered a healthful food for some, others have been frightened by the warning about the cholesterol in eggs.

3. Child-directed cereal advertisements, and morning rush, are more influential in determining what is for breakfast than the actual fact that eggs cook quickly and are low priced.

4. Some people think that eggs have too many calories in spite of the fact that they are relatively low in calories for the nutrients received.

Eggs are an excellent food, considered by some a "perfect" food. They rate high on the nutrition scale, being rich in protein and also supplying iron and vitamins A and B^2. Eggs contain an anticholesterol factor according to some research, and eaten several times a week by adults offer needed nutrients.

SIZE AFFECTS RECIPES

A warning about using eggs in recipes: Notice how the size of eggs used in a recipe can vary the actual quantity of eggs you put in. Because eggs do vary in

105

size and weight, you may be disappointed in a recipe if you use less than the minimum amount specified.

Always measure eggs in a measuring cup. You can generally depend on the following equivalents:

2 medium eggs = ⅓ cup   *3 medium eggs = ½ cup*
2 large eggs = ½ cup   *3 large eggs = ⅔ cup*

SCRAMBLED EGGS, MEXICAN

Break 4 eggs, one at a time into a saucer, then slip into a mixing bowl. Add ⅓ cup milk, 1 tablespoon soy oil, ⅛ teaspoon salt. Mix with a fork only enough to break up the eggs.

Place 2 tablespoons soy oil (or other seed oil) in frying pan over medium fire. Lightly brown 2 tablespoons minced onion and 2 tablespoons chopped green pepper. Pour in egg mixture. Cook over low heat, stirring only 2 or 3 times, until mixture is set. Sprinkle grated cheese over the top and serve. A dash of Tabasco sauce or 1 tablespoon chili sauce may be added to onions before adding eggs, if desired. Serves 3-4.

EGGS IN A FRAME

Pull out center from a slice of wholegrain bread or cut out center with a biscuit cutter. Butter bread generously on both sides. Brown "bread frames" on one side in hot oil or broiler. Turn over, drop egg into center.

Cook slowly in covered pan until egg white is set. Sprinkle lightly with sea salt; lift out with pancake turner and serve.

EGGS ITALIAN

3 tablespoons olive or other oil
1 onion
1 cup thinly sliced cooked Italian squash or sautéd mushrooms
2 fresh tomatoes

8 eggs
1 tablespoon Worcestershire Sauce
Salt and pepper to taste
Pinch of oregano
1 cup sharp natural cheese

Heat the oil in a large skillet and sauté the onion until brown. Add the squash and tomatoes. Cook slowly for about 10 minutes, stirring frequently. Remove from pan. Beat eggs and add seasonings. Stir the vegetable mixture into the eggs and pour back into frying pan. Cover and cook over low flame until the egg shrinks away from the sides of the pan. Remove from the fire, sprinkle with cheese and place pan at once under the broiler until cheese melts. Cut in wedges. Serves 6.

FRENCH EGGS

2 whole eggs
2 teaspoons water or milk

Butter
Salt and pepper

Break eggs into a bowl. Beat with a fork until well blended. Add water (or milk), salt and pepper. Mix well and pour into a pre-heated, well buttered pan. Do not stir. As the eggs cook, lift one edge of the omelet with a spatula and tilt pan so that the soft egg on top goes down to the bottom of the pan. Sprinkle any of the following on one half of the omelet; fold over and serve.

1. Sauted chopped tomatoes and chopped peppers in butter
2. Crumbled crisp bacon

107

3. Cooked minced onions in butter (but do not brown)

4. Chopped cooked mushrooms

5. Mixed herbs—chopped parsley, thyme, tarragon and chervil

6. Minced sprouts and finely chopped green onion tops

7. Grated Cheddar or Swiss cheese

8. Finely chopped leftover ham or other meat, mixed with sour cream

Note: Eggs, like all protein food, should be cooked at low heat. When cooking the omelet, have the heat very low, tipping the skillet so the uncooked' mixture flows evenly over the pan. Serves 2.

AVOCADO OMELET

4 eggs	*1 medium avocado, peeled*
4 tablespoons milk	*and chopped*
Dash of salt and pepper	*Paprika*
Butter or oil	

Break eggs into a bowl and beat with a fork. Add milk, salt and pepper. Pour into a hot buttered or oiled skillet. As egg cooks on the sides and on the bottom, lift omelet and tip skillet so that uncooked egg flows to the bottom of the pan. When it is firm, slide onto a platter. Cover one half with chopped avocado, fold over carefully. Sprinkle with paprika and serve at once. Serves 3-4.

SPANISH POTATO OMELET

This is a hearty breakfast dish; or it could be served when a quick meal is needed in the evening.

½ cup salad oil (not olive oil)
4 cups diced cooked potatoes, cooled, (have on hand)
1 small onion, chopped
Salt
¼ teaspoon cumin powder
8 eggs
⅓ cup milk
2 cups stewed tomatoes
¼ teaspoon sweet basil

Heat oil in a large skillet. Add potatoes, onion, ¾ teaspoon salt and cumin. Brown potatoes in the oil over high heat, turning them occasionally. Lower heat. Beat eggs with milk and pour over potatoes and mix lightly. Cover and cook over low heat, without stirring, 10 to 12 minutes or until omelet is set.

Meanwhile, pour tomatoes into saucepan. Break up pieces, add basil and salt to taste. Simmer uncovered 10 minutes. Loosen omelet with spatula and turn onto plate. Serve with stewed tomatoes. Serves 4-6.

EGGS AND WHOLE GRAIN RICE

This is a "quick to fix" dish, and with fruit and milk makes a good breakfast.

¼ cup butter
6 eggs
1 cup cooked brown rice
⅓ cup milk
½ cup chopped green onions
Salt to taste
½ cup chopped green pepper
1 tablespoon chopped parsley
½ teaspoon pepper
¾ cup shredded cheddar cheese

Melt butter in a large, heavy skillet. Beat eggs until frothy. Add rice, milk, onion, green pepper, parsley

109

and seasonings. Pour mixture into skillet. Cook, stirring constantly, until eggs are done. Serve with shredded cheese. Serves 4.

EGG SALAD MOLD

This is another good way to use up Easter eggs. You can use crab, shrimp or chicken instead of eggs.

1 envelope unflavored gelatin	1 cup finely diced celery
¼ cup cold water	¼ cup finely diced green pepper
½ teaspoon salt	¼ cup chopped cooked beets
2 tablespoons lemon juice	4 hard-boiled eggs, chopped
¼ teaspoon Tabasco sauce	
¾ cup mayonnaise	

Sprinkle gelatin on water in a 2½-quart saucepan to soften. Place over moderate heat, stirring constantly until gelatin is dissolved. Remove from heat; stir in salt, lemon juice, Tabasco and mayonnaise. Blend well. Chill, stirring occasionally, until mixture mounds when dropped from a spoon. Stir in remaining ingredients. Turn into a 3-cup mold. Chill until firm. Unmold and garnish with greens. Serves 4 to 6.

HAM AND EGG CASSEROLE

This dish can be made the day before and refrigerated until ready to cook. It could be served for breakfast or lunch.

6 tablespoons butter	1½ cups diced cooked ham (chicken could be used)
6 tablespoons flour	8 hard-boiled eggs, sliced
¾ teaspoon salt	3 tablespoons minced parsley
Dash of pepper	
½ teaspoon nutmeg	
3 cups milk	

Melt butter. Add flour and seasonings and blend together. Add milk gradually and cook until thickened, stirring constantly. Add diced ham, sliced eggs and chopped parsley. Fill 1½-quart casserole with creamed mixture. Sprinkle with paprika. Bake at 325° until bubbly (about 20 minutes). Serves 8.

LOLLIPOP EGGS

Place hard-boiled and peeled eggs in juice left over from pickling beets. Let them stand several hours or overnight in the refrigerator. Drain. Insert lollipop stick into end of each egg. Place in cellophane bag for school lunch box.

EGGS IN TOAST NESTS

4 slices wholegrain bread
2 tablespoons melted butter
4 eggs

4 teaspoons grated
   Parmesan cheese
Salt and pepper

Trim crusts from wholegrain bread. Press slices into well-oiled custard or muffin cups. Brush with butter. Break an egg into center of each slice. Season with salt and pepper. Sprinkle with cheese. Bake at 350°, 15 minutes or until eggs are set and bread lightly toasted.

EGG SALAD FOR SUMMER LUNCHEON

2 envelopes unflavored
   gelatin
¼ cup cold water
1 tablespoon curry powder

2 cups hot chicken broth
   (can use chicken concen-
   trate)
1½ cups mayonnaise
3 hard-boiled eggs, sliced
6 stuffed olives, sliced

Soften gelatin in cold water. Add gelatin and curry

powder to chicken broth, stirring to dissolve. Chill mixture until thick as unbeaten egg white. Gradually stir into mayonnaise until blended. Mix in sliced eggs and olives. Add salt if needed. Turn mixture into a 1-quart ring mold and chill until firm. Unmold on crisp greens and garnish with more sliced eggs and olives. Serves 6.

EGG-TUNA PIE

Butter well a 9-inch glass pie plate (you may use other pie pans). Beat 4 eggs, add ¼ cup milk, 1 can (6½ or 7 ounces) tuna (flaked), or other flaked fish, ½ pound grated Mozzarella cheese, ¼ teaspoon salt, ½ teaspoon basil, ½ teaspoon oregano. Spoon into well-buttered pie plate. Bake in hot oven (425°) until brown (do not boil), or until knife comes out clean (about 20 minutes). Serve hot in pie wedges. Mushroom or tomato sauce may be served on each piece. Serves 4.

EGGS BAKED IN TOMATO SHELLS

6 firm tomatoes　　　　*Buttered wholewheat*
Salt and pepper　　　　　　*crumbs*
6 eggs　　　　　　　　*Parmesan cheese*

Remove pulp from tomatoes to make shells. Sprinkle insides with salt. Drop an egg into each shell and top with bread crumbs and Parmesan cheese. Bake in muffin tins at 375°, for 25 minutes or until eggs are firm. Serves 6.

PICKLED EGGS

The juice from cooked beets makes fine pickled eggs. Into a 1-quart saucepan pour ½ to ¾ cup beet juice. Add 1 cup cider vinegar, ⅛ cup honey or dark brown sugar, 6 whole cloves, 1 stick cinnamon. Slowly bring to a boil, stirring a few times. Boil for 10 minutes. Remove the cloves and the cinnamon. Put the eggs in a 1-quart jar and pour the hot spiced mixture over them. Crumple transparent wrap over the eggs to keep them submerged. Cover and refrigerate overnight for mild-flavored, light-colored eggs, or for 2 to 4 nights for spicy-flavored dark-colored eggs.

TUNA-EGG-SOUP SANDWICH

Put 4 slices of buttered wholegrain toast on a cookie sheet; spread with 7 ounces of canned tuna drained, washed in lukewarm water, then flaked. Top tuna with minced onion and 2 slices of hard-boiled eggs. Mix mushroom or celery soup with ⅓ cup milk and 2 tablespoons chopped parsley; pour this over the sandwiches. Broil until heated through.

AVOCADOS WITH CHICKEN SALAD

2 cups cooked, boned,
  chicken, chopped
¼ cup chopped green
  pepper
1 medium orange, peeled
  and sectioned
¼ cup slivered almonds
¼ cup cooked salad dressing
  or mayonnaise
½ teaspoon salt
1½ tablespoons lemon juice
2 large ripe avocados
Salad greens

In a medium bowl, combine chicken, pepper, orange, almonds, salad dressing, salt and 1 tablespoon lemon juice. Mix well, Refrigerate, covered, until well chilled, at least 1 hour.

Just before serving, cut avocados in half lengthwise; remove pits. Sprinkle with remaining juice. Top each half with about ½ cup chicken salad, mounding high. Serve on crisp romaine. Serves 4.

AVOCADO MOUSSE

1 cup water
1 tablespoon unflavored gelatin (1 envelope)
3 cups mashed ripe avocado (about 3 or 4 medium ones)
½ cup mayonnaise
2 tablespoons lemon juice
2 tablespoons grated onion
1 teaspoon salt
1 teaspoon grated lemon peel
1 teaspoon prepared horse-radish
½ cup chilled heavy cream, whipped

Soften gelatin in ½ cup of the water in a saucepan; stir over low heat until gelatin is dissolved. Remove from heat and stir in the remaining ½ cup water. Set aside to cool.

Meanwhile, blend next 7 ingredients in a large bowl. Stir cooled gelatin into the avocado mixture. Chill until mixture begins to gel. Stir occasionally.

Fold in the whipped cream and turn into an oiled 5½-cup ring mold. Chill until firm. When ready to serve, unmold onto a chilled serving plate. Fill center of ring with large sprigs of watercress. Serves 12.

GREEK CHICKEN

This is one method of preparing a stewing chicken. Cut up one hen as for frying. Put pieces in a roasting pan. Add:

1 onion sliced
2 cloves garlic
¼ teaspoon allspice
¼ teaspoon marjoram
1 teaspoon cumin powder
1 teaspoon thyme
Dash of paprika
Salt and pepper to taste
1 can tomato sauce
1 cup tomato juice or tomatoes

Bake covered at 300°, for 3 or 4 hours until tender. Serve with freshly chopped parsley. Serves 4-6.

FRUIT PIE FOR EASTER

1 baked 9-inch pie shell
1 10-ounce package frozen
   red raspberries
1 12-ounce package frozen
   sliced peaches
2 tablespoons fresh lemon
   juice
2 tablespoons cornstarch or
   3 tablespoons arrowroot

2 oranges, peeled, cut into
   bite-size pieces, drained
1 large banana, sliced
1 large orange, peeled,
   sliced into cartwheels
½ cup heavy cream,
   whipped

Using your favorite oil pastry recipe, prepare 9-inch pie shell: bake and cool. Thaw raspberries and peaches. Drain and reserve juice.

To prepare glaze: In saucepan, stir lemon juice and cornstarch together; blend in drained fruit juice (there should be about 1¼ cups). Bring to boil, then reduce heat and simmer 4 to 5 minutes. Cool.

Combine drained raspberries, peaches, drained orange pieces and sliced banana; stir ⅔ of the cooked glaze through fruit. Spoon fruit into baked pie shell. Cut orange cartwheels in half and arrange on top of pie. Spoon remaining glaze over fruit.

Chill an hour or longer. Serve with whipped cream. Serves 6-8.

MINTED FRESH PINEAPPLE

Cut between shell and flesh to loosen pineapple. Remove fruit, cut out core and cut into cubes. Toss with ¼ cup orange juice and 1 tablespoon finely chopped mint leaves. Pile fruit into half shell and garnish with additional mint leaves. Serves 6.

HOW TO COOK WITH VANILLA BEAN

This slender wrinkly black bean, with its tiny fragrant

seeds, comes from the handsome flowers of an orchid plant. If it is new to you, experiment a bit, for it can add an exciting flavor bouquet to all kinds of sweet treats. Here are a few suggestions:

CUSTARD AND CREAM FILLING

Use a 1-inch long piece of vanilla bean for each cup of milk called for in your favorite recipe. Split the pod, scrape out the seeds with a spoon or knife, and place both pod and seeds in the milk, then scald. Let stand 5 minutes to develop the flavor; strain and prepare, following your recipe.

ICE CREAM

A 2-inch long piece of vanilla bean for each cup of milk or cream called for in your recipe gives a mellow just-right flavor. Scald with liquid, and strain, as for custard above.

VANILLA TRICKS

Drop the scraped pod into a box of raisins to flavor them; stir raisins into cookies, rice or bread puddings, or apple Betty. Same trick works equally well with coconut for sprinkling on a cake or fresh fruit cup.

CAKE AND COOKIES

A 1-inch piece of vanilla bean is enough for a regular 8 or 9-inch two-layer cake or a 3-dozen batch of cookies. Scrape the seeds from the split pod and add them to the sugar or honey and shortening as you're creaming them.

BEVERAGES

Have carob-flavored milk fans at your house: give them a treat by adding a few seeds of the vanilla bean to the milk as it's heating. They'll like the way this simple addition brings out the flavor.

May

HONEY—THE SWEETHEART OF THE KITCHEN
SPRING VEGETABLES

Orange Buttermilk Molds
Fluffy Honey Dressing
Honey French Dressing
Dried Fruit Torte
Apricot Cream
Honey Syrup
Freezing Peaches or Apricots
Herbs for Seasoning Vegetables
Herb Butter for Vegetables
Comfrey Fritters
Comfrey Casserole
Green Noodles for a Spring Dish
Dinner Ring
Individual Brown Rice Molds
Main Dish Cheese-Olive Souffle
Armenian Green Beans
Broiled Tomatoes
Quick Spanish Rice
Vegetable Rice Loaf
Cheese and String Bean Casserole
Chinese Peas

HONEY: THE SWEETHEART OF
THE KITCHEN

Honey is one of nature's sweetest products and incredibly versatile when it comes to uses in the kitchen.

Its use as a sweetening agent in place of sugar is obvious, but there are some other areas you may not have thought of—in salad dressings, for instance.

Honey comes in a great variety of flavors because bees are so well-traveled (they frequently travel as far as 400 miles from one pollinating location to another).

Many flavors are a result of blending by producers to keep a uniform flavor. Among the most popular are orange, clover, sage, mountain flowers, alfalfa and buckwheat. But no matter what the flavor, they all have one thing in common: they are pure honey.

Pure honey may be liquid (or extracted), creamed, comb or chunk. Liquid honey is clear and free flowing. Creamed honey is made commercially by introducing finely cyrstalized honey into liquid honey. Under controlled temperature conditions the honey is then agitated until it is creamy and spreadable. It does not require refrigeration. It is all honey with no drip.

A small amount of honey is sold in wooden frames as taken from the bee hive. This is comb honey. Chunk honey is honey comb in a jar with liquid honey filling up the spaces.

If the liquid honey you have granulates, it can be restored to liquid easily by heating in a pan of warm (not hot) water or placing the container in a very, very slow oven that has a temperature control set at no higher than 200°. Overheating destroys both color and delicate flavor. Granulated honey is not spoiled. It can be used as a spread or ingredient product for baked goods. All honey sweetened baked goods keep well and are tender and moist.

Keep honey in a dry place. Honey absorbs and retains moisture. Do not put honey in the refrigerator unless you wish to hasten granulation. Freezing does not injure the color or flavor of honey.

Substituting honey for sugar in recipes is easy. Replace equal amounts up to one cup and decrease liquid ¼ cup for each cup of honey used. Also reduce baking temperatures 25 degrees to prevent overbrowning. When using honey in cooking, measure the oil or liquid first, then measure the honey in the same cup or spoon. It will slide off with ease.

Honey makes a moist, tender product. A crisp cookie will not stay that way. To insure a tender and less crumbly cookie or cake add two tablespoons honey to your batter.

In addition to its sugars, honey contains as its minor components a number of minerals, seven members of the B-vitamin complex, ascorbic acid (vitamin C), dextrins, plant pigments, amino acids, other organic acids, traces of protein, esters and other aromatic compounds and several enzymes.

ORANGE BUTTERMILK MOLDS

1 envelope unflavored gelatin	⅛ teaspoon salt
½ cup orange juice	¾ teaspoon grated orange peel
1 egg, separated	1¼ cups buttermilk
⅓ cup honey	

Soften gelatin in orange juice in top of double boiler. Beat egg yolk lightly. Combine with gelatin and cook, stirring constantly, until gelatin dissolves and egg yolk thickens mixture slightly. Set aside 2 tablespoons of

122

the honey for the egg white. Stir remaining honey, salt, orange peel and buttermilk into gelatin mixture. Cool until gelatin thickens and begins to jell. Beat egg white stiff. Gradually beat in remaining honey. Fold into gelatin. Turn into individual molds and chill until firm. Serves 4 or 5.

FLUFFY HONEY DRESSING

2 *eggs*	⅛ *teaspoon salt*
½ *cup honey*	½ *cup yogurt or whipped*
¼ *cup lemon juice*	*cream*
2 *tablespoons frozen*	2 *teaspoons lemon peel*
orange juice concentrate	

Beat eggs. Stir in honey, lemon juice, orange concentrate and salt. Cook over low heat until thickened. Cool. Fold in yogurt or whipped cream and lemon peel. Serve with fresh fruit. Serves 4.

HONEY FRENCH DRESSING

1 *can (8 ounces) tomato*	¼ *cup lemon juice*
sauce	⅓ *cup honey*
1⅓ *cups salad oil*	1½ *teaspoons salt*
½ *cup cider vinegar*	2 *teaspoons paprika*

Combine all ingredients in glass jar with tight-fitting lid and shake until well blended. Chill. Shake well before serving. Makes about 3 cups.

DRIED FRUIT TORTE

2 *eggs*	¼ *cup pastry wholewheat*
⅓ *cup dates (cut up)*	*flour*
⅓ *cup figs (cut up)*	1 *cup chopped walnuts or*
⅓ *cup apricots (cut up)*	*pecans*

Beat whites and yolks of eggs separately. When beating whites, add 2 tablespoons water to make them less dry. Mix beaten yolks, fruits, flour and nuts. Fold into egg whites. Bake in buttered pan, set in hot water in moderate oven, 350° for ½ hour.

APRICOT CREAM

1 *cup sieved cooked dried apricots*
⅓ *cup honey*
½ *teaspoon salt*
2 *cups dairy sour cream*

Blend apricots, honey and salt into the sour cream. Chill for several hours or overnight before serving. Serve in sherbet glasses, garnished with toasted almonds or coconut. Serves 6.

HONEY SYRUP

Honey syrup may be made in quantity and stored in refrigerator ready for use.

Syrup for 6 large glass containers: Bring 1 quart water to boil, remove from heat, stir in 1½ cups honey, according to sweetness desired, into water until well mixed. Allow to cool before refrigerating.

FREEZING PEACHES OR APRICOTS

Set up freezer containers in assembly-line order. Pour ¾ cup cold honey syrup into each container.

Wash peaches quickly in cold water. Peel 1 peach at a time and slice directly into prepared syrup. Fill to 1 inch of top and be sure fruit is blended with syrup. Cover with piece of crumbled freezer wrap to keep fruit under syrup while freezing. Seal tightly with cover and freeze.

Apricots, if ripe, need not be peeled, only seeded and sliced.

HERBS FOR SEASONING VEGETABLES

(Snipped fresh, crumbled dried or ground herbs may be used.)

BASIL: Asparagus, Brussels sprouts, carrots, eggplant, green beans, tomato dishes, beets, cabbage, celery, peas, salad greens.

DILL: Cauliflower, tomatoes, green beans, wax beans, potato dishes, all softshell squashes, beets, cabbage, carrots, peas.

MARJORAM: Eggplant, green beans, soft-shell squashes, Swiss chard, carrots, limas, onions, peas, spinach.

OREGANO: Mushrooms, onions, tomatoes, cream sauce for any vegetable.

ROSEMARY: Split pea soup and casseroles, mushrooms, tomato sauces, spinach, turnips, potatoes.

SAVORY: Steamed cabbage, baked beans, any dried bean dish, stewed tomatoes, eggplant, hard shell squash.

TARRAGON: Add to melted butter for asparagus, green beans, Swiss chard, beets, celery, peas, spinach.

HERB BUTTER FOR VEGETABLES

¼ pound butter	1 teaspoon fresh or ¼
2 tablespoons lemon juice	teaspoon dried basil
1 teaspoon snipped chives	1 teaspoon fresh or ¼
	teaspoon dried marjoram

Heat butter with lemon juice, chives, basil and marjoram. Serve over Brussels sprouts or other vegetables. Makes 6 to 8 servings.

COMFREY FRITTERS

First make a regular batter of 1¼ cups wholewheat flour, 3 teaspoons baking powder, ½ teaspoon salt, 1 cup milk, 1 egg, 2 tablespoons oil, 1 teaspoon molasses or honey. (Extra batter may be used to make hot cakes).

Wash and dry the fresh comfrey leaves. Dip in the batter and saute in oil. Serves 4-6.

COMFREY CASSEROLE

2 eggs, beaten
2 cups milk
1 medium minced onion
1 clove minced garlic
¼ cup oil
½ teaspoon salt

2 cups cooked brown rice
½ cup chopped comfrey or spinach or parsley
1 cup grated cheddar cheese

Combine eggs, milk, onion, garlic, oil and salt. Place rice, comfrey and cheese in layers saving out some cheese for the top, in a buttered 1½-quart casserole. Pour the egg mixture over all, cover with cheese and bake at 350°, 40 minutes. Serves 4.

GREEN NOODLES FOR A SPRING DISH

If green noodles are not available, use regular noodles. Cook as directed on the package, or make your own noodles.

1 pound green cooked noodles (spinach used to color)
¼ cup oil
1 clove garlic, quartered

6 sprigs parsley (no stems)
1 teaspoon sweet basil
⅛ teaspoon pepper
½ cup grated Parmesan cheese

Combine oil, garlic, parsley, basil and pepper in blender. Blend for a few seconds at low speed until parsley is minced. Combine with noodles and heat slowly. Add cheese and toss. Serves 4 to 6.

DINNER RING

2 envelopes *unflavored* gelatin

1 can beef broth or ¾ cup broth (or beef concentrate)

1 can tomato juice or 2 cups tomato juice

½ teaspoon sea salt

2 tablespoons lemon juice

¼ teaspoon *Tabasco*

2 cups diced cooked chicken (or use shrimp, crab or tuna)

2 cups chopped celery

½ cup chopped cucumbers

½ cup sliced olives

Sprinkle gelatin on ½ cup of the beef broth to soften. Place over low heat and stir until gelatin is dissolved, 2 or 3 minutes. Remove from heat and stir in remaining beef broth, tomato juice, salt, lemon juice and Tabasco. Chill until mixture mounds slightly when dropped from a spoon. Fold in remaining ingredients. Turn into a 6-cup ring mold or other mold. Chill until firm. Serves 6 to 8.

INDIVIDUAL BROWN RICE MOLDS

Buy brown rice only, since it has just the hull removed. Polished white rice has had seven outer brown coatings removed, coatings which hold life-giving vitamins.

Place 2½ cups water in a heavy kettle or frying pan, bring to a boil and add ½ teaspoon of salt. Add 1 cup rice; stir to see that the rice has not stuck to the bottom of the pan. Cover tightly and turn to simmer or very low heat. Cook about 45 minutes. Do not remove cover during cooking. This rice should be dry and soft, with each grain separate.

When rice has cooked, pack in small, oiled glass custard cups and refrigerate. The next morning these rice molds may be turned out and served cold or placed in a steamer and steamed a few minutes until warm. Serves 6-8.

MAIN DISH CHEESE-OLIVE SOUFFLE

¾ cup uncooked brown rice
2½ cups water
1 teaspoon salt
2 tablespoons butter
2 tablespoons flour (un-
   bleached white)
1¾ cups milk

1 cup grated natural
   cheddar cheese
½ teaspoon salt
¼ teaspoon pepper
½ teaspoon nutmeg
4 eggs, separated
½ cup stuffed green olives,
   sliced

Put the rice, water and salt in 2-quart sauce pan. Bring water to a boil, turn the heat to low, cover with a tight lid and let simmer over low heat for 40 minutes. Do not remove lid for 35 minutes. While the rice cooks, melt the butter in a sauce pan. Blend in flour. Gradually stir in the milk. Cook, stirring several minutes. Stir in the cheese and cook, stirring constantly, until the cheese melts and the mixture thickens. Stir in salt, pepper and nutmeg. Beat the egg yolks. Stir in some of the hot cheese mixture. Return the egg yolk mixture to the saucepan.

After the rice cooks (there should be no water remaining) stir in the cheese sauce and olives.

Beat egg whites stiff but not dry. Fold in the rice-cheese mixture. Place in an ungreased 2-quart baking dish. Place in a pan of hot water in a preheated 350° oven. Bake for 1 hour or until a silver knife inserted in the center comes out clean. This will serve 6 to 8.

ARMENIAN GREEN BEANS

1 pound green beans,
  washed but not dried
2 tablespoons oil
1 tablespoon butter

1 cup fresh sliced mush-
  rooms (or 1 4-ounce can)
½ cup sour cream
¼ cup buttered bread
  crumbs

Remove ends and strings from beans. Cut into julienne
strips and cook in 2 tablespoons oil until barely
tender. Place in casserole. Sauté mushrooms in butter
and spread over beans. Cover with sour cream, then
crumbs. Dust with paprika. Bake at 375°, for 10 minutes or until crumbs are brown. Serves 4.

BROILED TOMATOES

6 medium sized tomatoes
Salt and pepper

2 tablespoons grated
  Parmesan cheese
1½ teaspoons butter

Halve tomatoes crosswise; sprinkle with salt and pepper. Then sprinkle about ¼ teaspoon Parmesan cheese
over each tomato half; dot each with butter. Broil for
4 to 5 minutes about 6 inches from broiler. Serves 6
with 2 halves each.

SPANISH RICE

¼ cup oil
1 yellow onion, thinly
  sliced
1 stalk celery with leaves,
  finely sliced
½ green pepper, diced
1 clove crushed garlic
1½ cups canned
  tomatoes, cut up

1½ cups cooked brown rice
1 teaspoon salt
Dash of cayenne
Cumin and chile powders to
  taste
½ cup grated cheddar or
  Monterey Jack cheese

Heat oil, and onion, celery, green pepper and garlic.
Cook and stir until slightly soft and lightly browned.
Add tomatoes and rice. Stir in seasonings and cheese.
Cover and bake in 350° oven for 45 minutes.

VEGETABLE RICE LOAF

2 cups cooked brown rice

2 cups wholegrain bread
crumbs

1 cup chopped nuts (pecans
or cashews)

4 tablespoons chopped
pimiento

¼ teaspoon oregano

2 tablespoons minced
onion

2 tablespoons finely
chopped green pepper

2 cups cooked or fresh
tomatoes

4 beaten eggs

1 teaspoon salt

Mix ingredients thoroughly, form a loaf and place in
oiled loaf pan. Bake 1 hour in moderate (350°) oven.
Serve with tomato sauce or sour cream. Serves 8.

CHEESE AND STRING BEAN CASSEROLE

4 cups fresh beans, cut up
or 3 packages frozen,
cooked until just tender

2 tablespoons butter or oil

2 tablespoons flour (pastry
wholewheat)

1 teaspoon salt

½ medium onion, grated

1 cup sour cream mixed
with ½ cup plain yogurt

½ pound gruyere or mild
Cheddar

½ cup wheat germ

Pinch sage

Melt butter in double boiler or over low heat. Stir in
flour, salt, sage and onion and cook, stirring, for 8-10
minutes. Remove pan from stove. Add sour cream,
and green beans. Pour into buttered casserole. Top
with grated cheese and wheat germ. Bake in 400°
oven about 20 minutes. Serves 6.

CHINESE PEAS

(String beans may substitute for peas in this recipe)

½ pound Chinese pea pods

1 tablespoon oil

½ cup thinly sliced water chestnuts or Jerusalem artichokes

Salt to taste

1 cup chicken broth

1 tablespoon cornstarch or arrowroot

2 tablespoons cold water

Snap off ends of peas and string pods, as you would green string beans.

Heat oil in a skillet, add pea pods, water chestnuts and broth. Cover and cook over high heat 3 minutes. Combine cornstarch (or arrowroot powder) and cold water. Spoon a little hot broth into mixture and blend. Push vegetables to one side of the pan and add cornstarch mixture to broth. Cook and stir only until lightly thickened. Combine with other ingredients. Serves 4.

Mix various vegetables for a different flavor. For example, carrots and celery, peas and onions, string beans and corn, zucchini and tomatoes. For a varied flavor add a few celery, dill or caraway seeds to the vegetables. Try dill with cabbage, caraway seeds on carrots, chives with peas and basil with tomatoes.

June

DAIRY MONTH; FRUIT JAMS

How To Whip Dry Skimmed Milk
Yogurt
Mock Sour Cream
Soy Cheese From Soy Flour
Fruit and Cheese Kabob Desert
Frosted Cheese Bars
Cottage Cheese Varieties For Dips
Cottage Cheese Molded Salad
Cottage Cheese and Broccoli Au Gratin
Fresh Coconut Cream Pie
Dessert Cheeses
Cream and Cheese With Strawberry Sauce
Strawberry Yogurt Parfait
Sour Cream and Applesauce
Yogurt Cheese
Angel Delight
Favorite Yogurt Pudding
Yogurt Pineapple Sherbet
Low Calorie Lemon Cake Top Pudding
Apricot Dessert
Custard Sauce
Orange-Grapefruit Honey Marmalade
Peach-Melon Marmalade
Apricot Jam Uncooked
Peach-Apricot Jam
Freezing Hints

JUNE—DAIRY MONTH

In recent years, eating habits in the United States have shown a definite downward trend, according to a report of a nation-wide survey of households which was conducted by the U.S. Department of Agriculture. The survey was made in the spring of 1965, when members of 7500 households, representative of the country as a whole, were interviewed. Also included in the report were 2500 families for each of the winter, summer and fall seasons, bringing the total households surveyed to 15,000.

The findings of the survey show that one household in every five (or 20 percent) eats a nutritionally "poor" combination of food, according to the standards of the U.S.D.A. In the previous survey made in 1955, only 15 percent were in this category.

The reason for the downward trend was ascribed primarily to the decreased use of milk and milk products, fruits and vegetables. While households are consuming less of these foods, they are consuming more ready-made baked goods and drinking more soft drinks. Comparative data shows a decrease in nutritive value of diets by 10 percent in calcium, 6 percent in thiamine, 4 percent in riboflavin, 10 percent in vitamin A and 5 percent in ascorbic acid.

Milk and milk products are among our best sources of calcium, B vitamins, vitamin A and protein and at reasonable cost. Milk also contains many enzymes, all of which are essential for its digestion.

The best milk is certified raw milk, and the community that can obtain it is most fortunate; but milk more readily available is also nutritious and valuable in the diet.

HOW TO WHIP DRY SKIMMED MILK

Mix ¼ cup cold water, 2 tablespoons lemon juice and 1 teaspoon vanilla in a quart bowl. Sprinkle ½ cup dry skim milk on top. Beat with rotary beater for 8 minutes; with electric beater for 4 minutes, or until mixture is stiff. Gradually beat in 3 teaspoons honey, continuing to beat about 2 minutes more until mixture resembles whipped cream. Chill 30 minutes to bring out flavor before serving. Makes 1½ cups.

YOGURT

It is absolutely necessary to use fresh yogurt culture (available at your health food store). Warm 2 quarts certified raw (if possible) or pasteurized milk to 115°; cool to 100° before adding starter.

Add 2 tablespoons yogurt for each pint of milk. Shake to break up solids. Pour into sterilized pint jars. Place in a large pan of warm water in oven. Keep oven temperature at 105°. Leave for 3 hours or until set. Refrigerate. If you want thicker yogurt, add ⅓ cup spray-dried powdered milk to each quart of yogurt before pouring into jars.

MOCK SOUR CREAM

Blend ½ cup creamed cottage cheese and ½ cup buttermilk until smooth. Add 2 teaspoons lemon juice and whirl a few seconds longer. Serve on fresh fruits, baked potato, fish or salads. Makes 1 cup. Chopped chives may be added, if desired.

SOY CHEESE FROM SOY FLOUR

Using 2 cups soy flour, make a paste with cold water. Add 1 quart boiling water. Set on a burner, over low heat. Stir mixture constantly until it boils, then simmer for 5 minutes. Watch carefully to see that the liquid does not burn. Remove from fire, add ½ cup apple cider vinegar. Let stand for 5 minutes. Pour into cheesecloth bag and squeeze.

This cheese can be eaten as is; or you may add seasonings such as onion, garlic, parsley, salt, pepper, horseradish, chopped olives or salad dressing.

FRUIT AND CHEESE KABOB DESSERT

Alternate cubes of cheese with chunks of fruit on wooden or metal skewers. Good combinations are pineapple chunks and Edam cheese, bananas with sharp American cheese, pears with Swiss cheese, grapes with jack cheese.

FROSTED CHEESE BARS

These are good in lunches or to serve as appetizers

1 8-ounce package cream cheese (you can use about 2 cups whipped cottage cheese)
¼ teaspoon prepared horseradish
½ teaspoon dry mustard
½ cup chopped toasted walnuts
¾ to 1 pound aged cheddar cheese

Beat cream cheese, horseradish and mustard until smooth. Stir in walnuts. Cut cheddar cheese into bars, circles or triangles. Frost one side of each piece with the walnut mixture. Cover and chill. Serves 6-8.

COTTAGE CHEESE VARIETIES FOR DIPS

Mix 1 carton cottage cheese, large curd, with any of the following:

1. 3 tablespoons each grated cheddar cheese, yogurt, mayonnaise, 2 tablespoons grated onion.

2. 2 tablespoons chopped almonds, ½ cup chopped dates, 2 tablespoons peanut butter.

3. Chopped red radishes, 2 tablespoons minced onion, ¼ cup minced parsley.

4. ¼ cup chopped tomato, ¼ cup minced parsley, 2 tablespoons minced onion, ¼ teaspoon cumin powder and salt to taste.

5. ½ cup alfalfa sprouts, 2 tablespoons mayonnaise, chopped walnuts (about ¼ cup).

6. ½ cup cut-up raisins, ¼ cup crushed pineapple, 1 teaspoon minced onion.

7. 2 hard-boiled eggs, chopped fine, ¼ cup celery, cut in thin slivers, seasonings to taste.

Note: Cottage cheese may be blended to the consistency of cream cheese. You may prefer to do this before mixing in the other ingredients for a dip. Fresh raw pieces of vegetables are preferred as dippers.

COTTAGE CHEESE MOLDED SALAD

1½ envelopes gelatin (1½ tablespoons)
⅓ cup cold water
3 cups cottage cheese (small curd)
1½ teaspoons salt
¼ teaspoon paprika
Dash of cayenne

3 tablespoons lemon juice
¾ cup light cream (or yogurt)
3 cups mixed, diced, drained fruit (bananas, oranges, grapes or any combination you desire)
½ cup salad dressing

Sprinkle gelatin on cold water. Combine cheese, seasonings, lemon juice, cream and dissolved gelatin; mix well. Turn into 1-quart ring mold which has been rinsed in cold water. Chill until set. Unmold on salad greens, Fill center of mold with the fruit. Serve with dressing. Serves 6.

COTTAGE CHEESE AND BROCCOLI AU GRATIN

1½ cups fresh broccoli, chopped and cooked (or 1 10-ounce package frozen)	¼ teaspoon pepper
	¼ teaspoon dill salt
	¼ teaspoon steak sauce
	1 teaspoon minced onion
1 cup cottage cheese	¼ cup melted butter
2 eggs, slightly beaten	¼ cup wholewheat bread crumbs
¼ teaspoon salt	

Cook and drain broccoli. Mix all ingredients except butter and crumbs. Stir in 2 tablespoons melted butter and pour mixture into buttered 8-inch pie plate. Mix butter and crumbs; sprinkle on top. Bake in 350° oven 30 minutes. Serves 4.

FRESH COCONUT CREAM PIE

1 envelope (1 tablespoon unflavored gelatin)	2 tablespoons butter
	½ teaspoon vanilla
1¾ cups milk	⅛ teaspoon almond flavoring
½ cup honey	
4 tablespoons arrowroot powder or	1 cup grated fresh coconut
	1 baked pastry shell (wholewheat)
2 tablespoons cornstarch	
½ teaspoon salt	½ cup whipping cream
2 eggs, separated	

Soften gelatin in ¼ cup milk. Blend honey, arrowroot and salt in medium-sized pan; gradually stir in remaining milk. Cook over low heat, stirring constantly, until mixture thickens and boils. Remove from heat, beat egg yolks slightly and stir a small amount of the hot liquid into the egg yolks. Add the egg-yolk mixture to the remaining hot milk mixture, return to the heat and continue cooking, stirring constantly, for 2 minutes.

Remove from heat and blend in the softened gelatin, butter and flavorings: cool until lukewarm.

Beat egg whites until stiff but not dry; fold egg whites with ¾ of the coconut into the cooled custard. Pour into pastry shell and chill.

Just before serving, whip cream; sweeten to taste and spread over coconut filling. Garnish with remaining coconut. Makes one 9-inch pie.

DESSERT CHEESE

Blue or Roquefort cheese is one of the most popular dessert cheeses. Camembert and Brie, Port du Salut, Edam or Gouda are all good selections to serve with fruit. No dessert is so sophisticated (and so simple to prepare) as fruit and cheese.

Any cheese you like is good on the dessert tray, but certain cheeses seem to team especially well with certain fruits: cheddar cheese is especially good with tart apples; team Swiss cheese with green grapes; blue or Roquefort is best with juicy pears; brick cheese with grapes, peaches and nectarines: Gouda or Edam cheese goes well with apples and pears; soft, ripened cheeses such as Camembert are good with grapes or spread on apple slices.

Be sure that the fruit is well-chilled and the cheese is room temperature.

CREAM AND CHEESE WITH STRAWBERRY SAUCE

Cream and cottage cheese base: whip ½ pint (1-cup) whipping cream and sweeten with 2 tablespoons honey. Stir in ½ pint creamed cottage cheese until well blended; chill until time to use.

Spoon half of the cream and cheese mixture in a parfait glass, cover with 2 tablespoons crushed sweetened (honey) strawberries. Add remaining cream/cheese mixture and top with ½ cup crushed fresh strawberries. Top with a large berry. Serves 4.

STRAWBERRY YOGURT PARFAIT

1 *cup plain yogurt*	*⅓ cup honey*
1 *tablespoon lemon juice*	2 *cups fresh strawberries*

Combine yogurt, honey and lemon juice in blender until smooth. Pour into ice cube tray and freeze until firm around the edges. Turn into chilled bowl and beat until smooth. Put back in tray and freeze until firm. Let stand at room temperature to soften slightly before serving, Alternate frozen yogurt and berries in parfait glass, topping with crushed berries. Ripe peaches may be used instead of berries. Serves 4.

SOUR CREAM AND APPLESAUCE

Blend equal amounts of sour cream and applesauce, adding a dash of cinnamon. Serve on hot cakes or French toast.

YOGURT CHEESE

1 *quart yogurt*
Place in cloth bag and hang overnight on faucet or other
   convenient place.
Add ¼ teaspoon salt.

After the whey has dripped through, the resulting yogurt cheese is delicious used as a spread instead of butter at breakfast. You may add crushed pineapple for variety.

ANGEL DELIGHT

Mix 1 cup of yogurt with ¼ cup rolled oats (uncooked) and 6 tablespoons honey.

Blend and put in refrigerator overnight. In morning add 1 cup coconut flakes, 1 cup seedless grapes, 1 cup pineapple bits and 1 cup mandarin orange slices or sliced peaches.

Mix in 1 tablespoon lemon juice, ¼ cup orange juice and ½ cup cashew nuts or ¼ cup sunflower seeds. Fold in ½ cup whipped cream; chill. Serves 4 to 6.

FAVORITE YOGURT PUDDING

Soften 1 tablespoon gelatin in ½ cup warm water. Put in blender 1 tablespoon sesame seeds and 1 tablespoon almonds. These can be ground in small mill first, then put in blender.

Add to ground nuts 1 pint yogurt, 1 tablespoon honey and 1 tablespoon vanilla. Blend for a few minutes. Fold in the gelatin. Pour into a mold and serve with pure maple syrup or crushed fruit. Serves 3-4.

YOGURT PINEAPPLE SHERBET

1 cup crushed pineapple   *½ pint vanilla yogurt*

Put yogurt in freezing tray and freeze slowly to soft mush. Remove and stir in crushed pineapple and juice. Return to freezing compartment and freeze to soft mush. Stir or beat well and freeze until solid. Vary by using sweetened mashed strawberries, raspberries or other berries, finely diced peaches, apricot juice or grape juice. Serves 2.

LOW CALORIE LEMON CAKE TOP PUDDING

3 tablespoons flour
¼ teaspoon salt
⅛ teaspoon nutmeg or mace
2 teaspoons softened butter
⅓ cup brown sugar

3 eggs, separated
½ teaspoon finely grated
  lemon peel
¼ cup fresh lemon juice
1¼ cups water

Sift flour, salt and nutmeg together; set aside. Mix butter and sugar, beating until light and fluffy. Add egg yolks one at a time, beating well after each addition. Fold in flour mixture, blending well. Add grated lemon peel, juice and water, mixing well. Beat egg whites until they hold in stiff peaks; fold lightly into lemon mixture. Spoon into custard cups filling each ¾ full. Place in shallow pan containing 1 inch hot water. Bake at 350°, for 30 to 35 minutes or until tops are firm. Calories: 130 per serving. Serves 4-6.

APRICOT DESSERT

Because of the expense of apricots use sparingly, but do enjoy the flavor. Cut up fresh apricots and serve with custard sauce. Sprinkle finely chopped walnuts over the top.

CUSTARD SAUCE

Heat 1½ cups milk in a double boiler. Beat 2 large or 3 medium eggs with 3 tablespoons honey and a pinch of salt. Add ½ cup of the heated milk a little at a time stirring well. Stir egg mixture into milk in double boiler and continue stirring steadily until custard coats spoon. Remove and flavor with almond or vanilla extract and chill. Serve over fruit.

ORANGE-GRAPEFRUIT-HONEY MARMALADE

4 medium size oranges,
  sliced thin
1 small, ripe grapefruit
6 cups water

9½ cups honey
½ cup lemon juice
3½ ounces commercial
  pectin

Slice oranges very thin and discard the end sections. Cut grapefruit in very small pieces. Add water and lemon juice to fruit, simmer in large pan until very tender, about 1 hour. Measure the cooked ingredients. Add additional water to make total cooked peel and juice exactly 7 level cups. Add pectin and bring to a boil. Add honey, gradually stirring until mixture returns to a rolling boil. Boil exactly 4 minutes. Remove from heat, skim and stir for 5 minutes. Pour into prepared glasses. Cover tightly with pliofilm. Refrigerate. Makes about 16 glasses. Paraffin is a coal tar product and I do not recommend it.

PEACH-MELON MARMALADE

3 cups cantaloupe cubes
2 cups fresh peach cubes
¼ cup lemon juice

3 cups mild flavored honey
1 cup coarsely chopped
  walnuts

Cut cantaloupe in half. Remove seeds and rind. Cut meat in cubes. Peel peaches, remove pits, cube. In a large kettle, combine fruit with lemon juice and honey. Bring to a boil, then cook over medium heat. Stir frequently to prevent sticking until fruit is clear and mixture thickens to consistency of marmalade. Remove from heat, skim and stir for 7 minutes; add walnuts. Ladle into sterilized jelly glasses and seal at once. Makes about six 8-ounce glasses. Marmalade becomes thicker on standing. Honey marmalade is never as thick as regular marmalade. Delicious over cooked rice, tapioca pudding or ice cream.

APRICOT JAM—UNCOOKED

Soak 1 cup dried apricots in enough hot water to just cover, for 3 hours or until water is absorbed and apricots soft. Chop apricots fine or put through medium blade of meat grinder. Mix with ¼ cup creamed honey (available at health food store) and ½ teaspoon grated lemon peel. Makes 1 cup.

PEACH-APRICOT JAM

Soak 1 cup dried apricots and 1 cup dried peaches in water to cover, for about three hours. Water should all be absorbed. Put through grinder or blender and mix with the juice of one lemon and a dash of salt. Heat with ½ cup creamed honey, stirring until thick.

SOME FREEZING HINTS

1. Buy cranberries when least expensive (usually November) and freeze. If kept frozen hard they will last all year.

2. Freeze persimmons when ripe for a taste treat. They can be frozen whole or peeled. Place in container without sweetener or ascorbic acid.

3. Separate egg; put yolk on oiled cake pan and freeze. Several yolks can go on one pan. When frozen take up with spatula and place in container. The whites can be put in small bags, 2 or 3 to a bag and frozen. Eggs can be frozen whole if beaten up first.

4. Bananas take on new flavor and texture when frozen. Freezing sweetens them and brings out their delicate flavor and aroma. Plain frozen bananas served whole are excellent. They can also be dipped in carob syrup, allowed to harden and then frozen. To make banana sherbet, simply mash and freeze. Serve alone or with nuts or yogurt preparation. Use thor-

oughly ripe bananas. Bruised areas need not be cut out if only a little darkened. Peel, place in pliofilm bags, exhaust all air and seal immediately. This will prevent discoloration. Refrigerator chill and place in coldest part of freezer for fast freezing. Bananas are not thoroughly ripe until the skin is well freckled. Freeze only fully ripe bananas.

5. Scoop out melon balls with ½ teaspoon measuring spoon; freeze for a treat in the winter.

6. To freeze whole peaches without syrup: wash firm, ripe fruit. Put single layer on cookie sheet and freeze. When solidly frozen store in plastic bags. To serve while still partially frozen, hold fruit under cold running water and gently wash the skin away. Slice and use like fresh fruit. Berries and cherries may be frozen this same way.

July

EATING OUTDOORS

Compact Kitchen and Ice Chest
Salad for First Day Camping
Fruit Medley
Cottage Cheese Stuffed Cantaloupe Salad
Fruit en Brochette
Custard Fruit Bowl
Fresh Peach Ice Cream
Hearty Beverages for Summer Snacks and Other Occasions
Buttermilk Lemonade
Carob-Banana Milk Shake
Crimson Cooler
Ambrosia Milk Shake
Pep Cocktail
Lunch Box Orange-Nog
Carob Milk
Carob Syrup
Malts With Frozen Milk
Carob Milk Shake
Comfrey Tea
Pink Cup
Herb Teas
Sesame Seed Milk
Luncheon Milk Shakes
Soya Milk Banana Shake
Spicy Punch

EATING OUTDOORS

The American people move outdoors in July because outdoor eating has become a summer tradition to which all the family looks forward.

The family will probably choose to eat in a patio, on a porch, near a backyard barbecue or to have a picnic any one of a dozen places in order to have a change from the winter's routine and to be out of doors.

Wherever the place may be, it is important that the cook plan ahead, so that she can enjoy the fun too.

There are some tricks in planning the summer meals which make summer cooking easier. Dinner can be prepared in the early morning before the heat becomes intense. You can prepare greens for salads, make gelatin salads such as jellied chicken or veal, and make a meat loaf. The meal can be refrigerated, so that it is ready to be warmed up or to be served.

When preparing casseroles, sandwiches, hors d'oeuvres and meats, you can cook an extra amount and freeze them.

If you always have a good supply of fresh fruits and vegetables, you can quickly make a salad which is the basis of the meal. Salad meals are a short cut because most of the ingredients can be prepared ahead of time and kept chilled.

There was a time when thick steaks and chops sold only in cold weather, but now they are the most popular cuts in warm weather with the advent of the barbecue, electric skillet and griddle. Keep a supply of hardwood chips such as hickory handy, so that at the whim of the family, steaks or hamburgers can be

149

grilled. (Wood chips are the safest fuel; charcoal and charcoal burnt food contain carcinogenic agents.)

Keep a picnic basket packed—with only food to be added, so that a picnic can be taken without too much advance notice.

Outdoor eating today is far more than just picnicking, it has a tremendous psychological affect toward good digestion and better health by insuring a relaxed atmosphere in which to eat a leisurely meal.

COMPACT "KITCHEN"
FROM MY FRIENDS, THE CLIFTONS

"We have dedicated one large piece of our luggage for use as our kitchen. It contains an electric table oven, 8x12 inches, which toasts, broils and bakes up to 500°; a one-pint electric percolator for heating water for hot drinks; paper plates, cups, napkins, towels; silverware and a paring knife. A variety of food can be taken and you will judge the amount according to the number of people you are preparing for and the number of days you plan to be away. We always take freshly baked bread, a jar of honey, salt, dates, nuts, peanut butter, fresh organically grown fruit in season, home-baked wholewheat cookies and cheese which will be used during the last part of the trip. This bag is securely locked so no unfortunate spill will occur."

ICE CHEST

"In addition to this piece of luggage (which no one suspects contains so much good eating!) we have begun taking a styrofoam ice chest containing the following, to be eaten during the first part of the trip: A jar of cooked ground steak or roast (ground for easy serving), a jar of cooked beans or peas, creamed potatoes or whole boiled potatoes, a plastic bag filled with fresh lettuce, tender greens, radishes, celery from the garden, a large jar of alfalfa sprouts, a jar of butter, a jar of homemade mayonnaise or dressing and a jar of freshly made museli for breakfast.

"I have also learned from experience that ice will last longer if you freeze it in your home deep freezer. I use an enamelware pan with lid for the container in which to make the ice. The lid is convenient in that I can place items directly on top of the ice."

SALAD FOR FIRST DAY CAMPING

Here is a salad to be eaten the first day on the road: Cut tops from 4 medium ripe tomatoes. Scoop out pulp, and sprinkle inside with salt; turn upside down and drain. Peel and dice 1 large cucumber. Season with chopped fresh dill; moisten with French dressing. Fill the tomatoes with the cucumber. Roll in cellophane and place in ice chest.

FRUIT MEDLEY

Another delicious combination to be used the first day of your trip is as follows:

½ honeydew melon, peeled and diced	2 cups seedless grapes
	Fresh mint
2 cups cantaloupe balls	¼ cup salad oil
2 cups fresh raspberries	¼ cup lime juice

Combine fruits and mint. If you wish to use these fruits as a salad, use the oil and lime juice; otherwise, take a small carton of yogurt to add dabs when fruits are served as a dessert. Serves 4-6.

COTTAGE CHEESE STUFFED
CANTALOUPE SALAD

3 small cantaloupes
2 cups cottage cheese
1 cup berries

1 cup fresh pineapple
  wedges
Mint sprigs

Cut melons in half lengthwise and scoop out seeds. Put on plates and fill centers with cheese and top with berries and pineapple. Garnish with mint. Serve with yogurt or sour cream. Serves 6.

FRUIT EN BROCHETTE

Place on long skewers and alternate, 1-inch piece of banana, half of a ripe apricot, chunk of fresh pineapple and large grapes.

Brush fruit with honey and sprinkle with ground walnuts. Broil 5 inches from fire until golden brown. Baste again while broiling, adding more nuts if desired.

Here are some fruit combinations for appetite starters.

1. Pineapple wedges cut from fresh pineapple, orange sections, grapes and bananas, then put all back into pineapple shell to serve. Cut pineapple shell into fourths.
2. Grapefruit and avocado pieces in tangy ketchup and cocktail sauce.
3. Grapefruit and orange sections with diced fresh pears and apple pieces. Pour on a little French dressing.
4. Cubed pineapple and papaya with orange sections and sour cream.
5. Chopped melon pieces or balls, blueberries and red-skinned apple wedges. Add a scoop of yogurt.

6. Cut up apricots, grapes, watermelon chunks and pineapple served with mint yogurt.
7. Fill halves of cantaloupe with raspberry juice gelatin cut into quarters.

CUSTARD FRUIT BOWL

3 *large oranges, pared and sliced*
2 *ripe bananas, peeled and sliced*
1 *cup fresh pineapple chunks or 1 can (13 ounces) frozen pineapple chunks, partly thawed*
1 *cup fresh mixed fruits such as peaches, pears and grapes*
½ *cup coconut*
Custard sauce

Arrange fruits according to kind in a large shallow glass bowl. Drizzle juice from oranges over bananas and peaches to keep them from discoloring. Sprinkle coconut over all. Chill. To serve, spoon fruits into individual dessert dishes. Top with cold custard sauce.

To make the custard sauce, combine 2 cups light cream or half-and-half, 1 cup milk, 1 tablespoon honey and 3 lightly beaten eggs in the top of a double boiler. Cook over hot water, stirring constantly until thickened. Remove from heat, add 1 teaspoon vanilla and ⅛ teaspoon nutmeg. Chill. Serves 4-6.

FRESH PEACH ICE CREAM

Thoroughly chill 2 cups of cream (or 1 large can of evaporated milk). Beat with rotary beater until cream stands in peaks.

Mash enough fresh raw peaches to make 1 cup. Add: 1 tablespoon lemon juice, 1 teaspoon almond flavoring and enough honey to sweeten to taste.

Carefully fold peach mixture into the whipped cream. Pour into refrigerator trays and freeze until firm. Serve topped with slices of fresh peach if desired. Serves 4-6.

HEARTY BEVERAGES FOR SUMMER SNACKS

1. Buttermilk lemonade: Blend 1 quart buttermilk, ½ cup lemon juice, 2 tablespoons honey and 2 teaspoons vanilla. Taste for sweetness. Serve cold.
2. Carob-banana milk shake: Mix in blender for only a few seconds 2 cups milk, ½ cup powdered milk, 2 tablespoons carob syrup, 1 sliced banana, ⅛ teaspoon salt. Serves 2.
3. Crimson cooler: Blend equal parts of tomato juice and buttermilk. Add a dash of thyme or basil.
4. Ambrosia milk shake: Mix ½ cup each, orange juice and apricot nectar, and ¼ cup honey. Blend in 1 cup milk and ¼ cup spray-dried powdered milk. Serve in chilled glasses. Serves 1 or 2, depending on size of glasses.

PEP COCKTAIL

2 tablespoons sunflower
seeds
6 almonds with skins
1 teaspoon wheat germ
1 teaspoon rice polish

¼ cup powdered skim milk
1 teaspoon honey
1 cup unsweetened pineapple juice or orange juice

Grind or blend sunflower seeds and almonds until fine. Add remaining ingredients and blend until smooth. Chill if desired. Makes one large glassful. Serves one.

LUNCH BOX ORANGE-NOG

1 egg
1 cup fresh orange juice,
well chilled

1 tablespoon brown sugar
Sprinkle ground cinnamon

154

Beat egg well. Add orange juice, brown sugar and cinnamon; mix well. Pour over ice cubes; stir until very cold. Put into well chilled vacuum bottle. Shake well before drinking. Serves 2.

CAROB MILK

2 cups cold fresh milk
4 tablespoons carob syrup
4 tablespoons powdered
   milk

Pinch of salt
½ teaspoon vanilla

Beat until smooth. Serve in chilled glasses. Serves 2.

CAROB SYRUP

¼ cup carob powder
⅓ cup honey
Pinch of salt

⅔ cup water
½ teaspoon vanilla

Mix honey and carob powder. Add water and salt. Boil 5 minutes. Add vanilla.

MALTS WITH FROZEN MILK

Freeze milk (certified raw if possible) in an ice cube tray.

Fill blender with cubes to the top; add ½ cup liquid milk (a little more if necessary depending on thickness). Add flavoring and dates, strawberries or bananas. Mix until blended, add honey if needed. This makes a very thick malt. Serves one.

CAROB MILK SHAKES

3 tablespoons carob
    powder
1 tablespoon powdered
    skim milk (not the instant
    kind)

1 or 2 tablespoons brown
    or raw sugar or honey
4 cups milk
½ teaspoon smooth peanut
    butter
½ ripe banana

Combine carob powder, powdered milk and sweetener with 1 cup milk. Place in blender; mix well. Add liquid milk, peanut butter and banana. Blend thoroughly. Serve hot or cold. For eggnog, add 2 well beaten egg yolks. Serves 3-4.

COMFREY TEA

Place 1 cup dried comfrey leaves in 3 quarts water. Bring to a boil, stir leaves, remove from fire. Cover tightly and steep over night. Next morning strain into glass jars and refrigerate. Very refreshing. Tastes like regular tea.

PINK CUP

1 12-ounce can vegetable
    juice, chilled

1 tablespoon dairy sour
    cream

Gradually blend vegetable juice into sour cream. Makes 3 to 4 servings.

HERB TEAS

Favorite combinations:

Mint-oat straw   *Strawberry-oat straw*
Cammomile-cinnamon stick   *Sassafras-hot or cold with*
Rose hip-alfalfa-mint   *lemon rind*
Juices—nutrients (especially enzymes) are largely lost when juices are canned or bottled. Use fresh fruit and vegetable juices whenever possible.

SESAME SEED MILK

½ cup sesame seeds   1½ cups water

Blend at high speed for 3-4 minutes. Strain through cheese cloth.

LUNCHEON MILK SHAKE

To 1½ cups cold milk, soy milk or yogurt, add 2 or 3 (or more) of the following foods and blend in a blender:

(If nuts or seeds are to be included, they must be run through before adding the other foods. If a blender is not available, use an egg beater. Grind the nuts and seeds before adding.)

½ cup orange juice or pineapple juice
½ cup skim milk powder
¼ cup dried whey
¼ cup powdered yeast
1 banana, mashed
1 apple peeled, cored and grated (or blended)
½ cup fresh fruit—peaches, apricots or berries

¼ cup fresh grated coconut (or powdered)
a few almonds, piñon nuts or cashews
¼ cup sunflower or sesame seeds
¼ teaspoon vanilla
1 or 2 eggs separated. Whites beaten stiff and folded in before serving.

Serves 2 or 3. Chill until ready to serve, and chill glasses in which drink will be poured.

A thermos bottle will keep this drink cold for the Lunch Box. No dessert is necessary with this drink.

SOYA MILK BANANA SHAKE

In a blender place 2 tablespoons soya powder and 1 pint water. Blend. Add 1 large banana, cut up, 1 tablespoon honey and ½ teaspoon vanilla. Blend again until well mixed. Serve. This can be made in a bowl using an egg beater and mashing the banana before adding to the soya milk. Serves 2.

SPICY PUNCH

PART I
1 cup cold water
⅓ cup honey
⅛ teaspoon salt
⅛ teaspoon ground nutmeg
6 whole cloves
4 2-inch pieces stick-cinnamon

PART II
3 tablespoons alfalfa tea
4 cups cold water
¼ to ⅓ cup apple concentrate

Combine all ingredients of part I in a sauce pan having a tight-fitting cover. Place over low heat, cover and let simmer for 20 minutes. Remove from heat, strain and set aside to cool. Chill thoroughly.

Bring 2 cups cold water to a full rolling boil in a sauce pan. Remove from heat and immediately add the tea (part II), stir. Let tea brew, uncovered, 5 minutes. Stir and strain into a pitcher containing the remaining cold water. Blend in the spiced syrup and apple concentrate. Serve with thin slices of orange. Will make 6 to 8 cupfuls.

August

SALADS

Tabuli
Main Dish Salad
Chef's Salad
Raw Vegetable Salad
Raw Vegetable Luncheon Salad
Molded Watermelon Fruit Salad
Basic Chicken Salad
Party Celery Dip
Celery Pinwheels
Marinated Celery
Avocado in Tomato Aspic
Avocado Gelatin Salad
Tomato Jelly Salad
Honey Waldorf Salad
Pear Salad
Cream-Herb-Potato Salad
Chicory With Hot Dressing
Summer Salad
Fresh Green Salad
Italian Salad
Low-Calorie Mushroom Salad
Asparagus Salad
Fresh Spinach Salad
Sprouted Alfalfa Salad
New Potato-Alfalfa Sprout Salad
Bean Sprout Salad
Three Bean Salad
Marinated Bean Salad
Carrot-Sesame Slaw
Grape Cole Slaw
Apple Slaw
Cheese Caraway Cole Slaw

159

Watermelon Compote
Melon Ball Fruit Cup
Mayonnaise
Alberta's Salad Dressing

SALADS

Raw fruits and vegetables, some nutritionists say, should comprise 50 percent of our diet. August is the time to exercise this practice—when summer gardens are producing their best and the weather discourages hot cooking and hard work. Growing your own organic salad makings is the most rewarding way to get them—but if you have no garden available, good fruits and vegetables are still to be found in markets or at summer stands. Salads are a refreshing way of life for both cook and family.

TABULI

This is excellent served with a cold meat platter or a baked bean casserole.

1 cup Bulgar wheat (from a 1-pound package purchased at a health food store)
1 large tomato, peeled and chopped
½ cup chopped fresh parsley
½ cup chopped fresh mint
1 medium-size onion, chopped
½ cup olive oil
¼ cup lemon juice
1 teaspoon salt
¼ teaspoon pepper
romaine

Place cracked wheat (Bulgar) in a medium-size bowl; cover with boiling water. Let stand 2 hours; drain well. Add tomato, parsley, mint and onion. Combine all remaining ingredients, except romaine, in a jar with a tight-fitting lid; shake well to mix. Pour over wheat mixture and toss lightly. Chill 2 hours. Serve over bite-size pieces of romaine. Serves 6.

MAIN DISH SALAD

1 10-ounce package frozen vegetables or 2 cups freshly cooked vegetables	1 tablespoon vinegar
	2 teaspoons grated onion
	½ teaspoon dry mustard
1½ cups cooked brown rice	1 cup diced ham or cooked, chopped chicken
¾ cup mayonnaise	
2 tablespoons oil	¾ cup diced celery

Drain vegetables well after cooking. Combine mayonnaise, oil, vinegar, onion, mustard, salt and pepper to taste. Combine cold vegetables, meat and celery in a bowl, then stir in dressing. Add rice and mix lightly. Chill salad 1 hour before serving. Serve on chopped lettuce. Serves 4.

CHEF'S SALAD

Rub salad bowl with clove of garlic. In the bowl place head lettuce and Romaine, torn into pieces, ½ cup chopped green onions, ½ cup thinly sliced celery and radishes, 1 cup of match-like sticks of Swiss cheese and cold cooked meats, such as ham, tongue, chicken. Keep very cold and just before serving toss a mixture of ½ cup sour cream and ¼ cup French dressing. Mayonnaise may be used instead of sour cream. Anchovies may be used as garnish if desired. Serves 6-8.

RAW VEGETABLE SALAD

On a bed of shredded romaine lettuce and water-cress place the following vegetables:

Cucumbers—sliced
Tomatoes—quartered
Celery—sliced very thin
Radishes
Carrot curls
White turnips—peeled and sliced very thin

Few tender young peas
Few cauliflower pieces
Chives or young onions—chopped fine and sprinkled over all

Add cheddar cheese in slender matchstick pieces. Slice avocado and add just before serving. Pour a well-seasoned French dressing over all.

RAW VEGETABLE LUNCHEON SALAD

Grate 3 small beets, 2 or 3 small carrots, 1 small head of cabbage, 1 or 2 sweet turnips and 2 or 3 peeled, grated parsnips sprinkled with lemon juice. Fringe (peel and draw fork down sides) and slice 1 cucumber. Cut 8 or 10 sticks of celery and 8 or 10 radish roses. Place small bib lettuce cups on 6 dinner plates. Put small serving of grated vegetables on each cup and a whole tomato (cut from center to represent a rose) in middle of plate. Alternate grated vegetables with celery, radishes and cucumbers. Pour small amount of French dressing on grated vegetables. Fill center of tomato with yogurt, mayonnaise or sour cream. Sprinkle chopped black olives on top. Serves 4-6.

MOLDED WATERMELON FRUIT SALAD

3 envelopes unflavored
gelatin
¾ cup cold water
4 cups diced watermelon
6 tablespoons fresh lemon
juice

½ teaspoon salt
1 cup small cantaloupe
balls
1 cup diced peaches
½ cup fresh blueberries or
strawberries

Soften gelatin in cold water. Place over hot water—
not boiling—to melt. Press watermelon cubes through
a sieve, measure juice. Add lemon juice, salt, and
softened gelatin. Mix well. Chill until mixture begins
to thicken, fold in fresh fruit. Pour mixture into a 6-
cup mold which has been rinsed with cold water.
Chill until firm. Serve with greens and mayonnaise or
yogurt. Serves 8.

BASIC CHICKEN SALAD

2 cups diced cooked
chicken
1 cup diced celery
¾ cup mayonnaise

1½ tablespoons lemon juice
¾ teaspoon salt, dash of
pepper
Lettuce or other greens

Toss chicken and celery. Mix together mayonnaise,
lemon juice, salt and pepper. Lightly toss chicken
mixture with dressing. Chill. Serve on salad greens.
One-half cup chopped green or black olives may be
added; also 2 chopped hard-boiled eggs and a few
almonds. Serves 4.

PARTY CELERY DIP

Raw vegetable salad used as a dip.

1 pound cream style cottage cheese	2 tablespoons finely chopped chives
1 teaspoon seasoned salt	½ cup minced green pepper
½ cup finely chopped celery	½ cup finely grated carrot
	Cucumber and celery sticks

Combine cottage cheese and seasoned salt. Beat until smooth with an electric mixer. Stir chopped celery, chives, green pepper and carrots into cottage cheese. Chill. Serve as a dip with cucumber and celery sticks. Serves 4-6.

CELERY PINWHEELS

Separate crisp celery stalks; wash, dry and stuff with pimiento cheese. Press stalks together, overlapping as celery grows. Tie with cord, wrap in cellophane bag. Chill for several hours until cheese is firm. Slice in half-inch-thick pinwheels with a sharp knife.

MARINATED CELERY

If possible, buy 2 bunches of the small trimmed celery stalks. Wash stalks but do not break apart. Cut them into quarters or eighths, depending on the size of the stalks. Steam until tender. Place in rectangular, glass baking dish. Pour the following marinade over stalks and marinate overnight.

Mix together ½ cup olive or salad oil, ½ cup cider vinegar, 1 teaspoon salt, ¼ teaspoon freshly ground pepper, ¼ teaspoon crumbled parsley, 1 clove garlic, cut into quarters, 2 tablespoons drained capers.

165

AVOCADO IN TOMATO ASPIC

2 cups tomato juice
½ bay leaf
½ teaspoon salt
1 stalk celery and leaves
1 envelope unflavored
  gelatin

¼ cup cold water
1 tablespoon onion juice
1 tablespoon vinegar
1 avocado peeled and
  cubed

Boil together for 10 minutes, the tomato juice, bay leaf, salt, stalk and leaves of celery. Sprinkle gelatin on top of cold water and add to hot mixture. Stir until gelatin is dissolved.

Add onion juice and vinegar. Strain and cool. When it begins to set, add the celery, chopped, and avocado. Allow to set firmly. Garnish with parsley and black olives. Serves 4-5.

AVOCADO GELATIN SALAD

⅓ cup cold water
2 envelopes unflavored
  gelatin
¾ cup boiling water
Juice of 1 lemon
Dash of Tobasco sauce
½ teaspoon salt

⅛ teaspoon pepper
1 teaspoon onion juice
2½ cups mashed avocado
  (2 or 3)
1 cup sour cream
1 cup salad dressing

Soften gelatin in cold water, then dissolve in the boiling water. Add the lemon juice, Tobasco sauce, salt, pepper and onion juice. Cool. Stir in mashed avocado, sour cream and salad dressing. Blend well. Pour into 1½-quart mold. Chill until firm, then unmold. Garnish with watercress and stuffed olives. Serves 6-8.

TOMATO JELLY SALAD

Basic Jelly

2 tablespoons granular
    gelatin
½ cup juice from the 3½
    cups canned tomatoes to
    be used

4 tablespoons lemon juice
Few grains of salt (to taste)

Cut up the tomatoes. Strain off ½ cup juice and soak gelatin in juice 5 minutes.

Heat remaining tomatoes and add softened gelatin. Stir until gelatin dissolves. Add salt and lemon juice. Allow to thicken, then if you wish, add 2 tablespoons chopped onion, ¼ cup chopped celery and leaves, 2 tablespoons chopped parsley, ½ cup grated carrot. If avocados are available, add 1 or 2 peeled and cut up.

Pour into molds and chill until firm. Serve with sour cream, to which has been added 2 or 3 tablespoons Roquefort cheese (crumbled). Serves 6-8.

HONEY WALDORF SALAD

1 cup chopped raw apple
1 cup thinly sliced celery
½ cup coarsely chopped
    walnuts

2 tablespoons honey
2 tablespoons sour
    cream
½ teaspoon salt

Toss all ingredients together lightly. Chill. Heap on crisp greens. Garnish with walnut halves. Serves 6.

PEAR SALAD

½ fresh unpeeled pear
top with cottage cheese
cover well with grated fresh coconut

Looks like coconut cupcake and tastes delicious as a salad.

CREAM-HERB-POTATO SALAD

Bake or steam enough potatoes to make 4 cups when cubed.

Combine the following, being careful not to mash the potato while mixing:

1½ teaspoons salt
⅛ teaspoon celery seed
1 medium onion, minced
½ teaspoon paprika
Enough sour cream to
  moisten well

1 tablespoon chopped fresh dill
2 tablespoons minced fresh parsley
6 sliced radishes
3 hard-boiled eggs cut in slices

After tasting you may wish to add 2 or 3 tablespoons apple cider vinegar. Chill and take to picnic in covered dish. Serves 4-6.

CHICORY WITH HOT DRESSING

4 slices bacon
¼ teaspoon paprika
¼ teaspoon salt
¼ teaspoon dry mustard
3 small white onions or six scallions
¼ teaspoon freshly ground pepper

3 tablespoons apple cider vinegar
1 teaspoon honey
2 tablespoons boiling water
1 head of chicory

Cut bacon (scissors are best) into small pieces and fry slowly. Dice 3 small white onions or six scallions and saute in bacon fat. Pour out all but 3 tablespoons of fat. Add seasonings, vinegar and honey dissolved in the hot water. Pour over large bowl of cleaned chicory and toss. Serve at once. Serves 4-6.

SUMMER SALAD

1 medium head of Boston lettuce washed and leaves torn into pieces
½ pound spinach washed and torn into bite size pieces
1 bunch watercress washed and torn into small sprigs (remove coarse stems)

¼ pound young tender zucchini, washed
1 cup thin onion rings
½ cup sliced fresh mushrooms or one 3-ounce can of sliced mushrooms drained
1 cup raw grated beets or cooked pickled beets
French dressing

Refrigerate greens in crisper until ready to use. With waffle-vegetable cutter, slice zucchini thinly crosswise or grate on coarse grater. Toss all together; serves 8.

FRESH GREEN SALAD

Fold together tender young spinach, chard and any other tender young greens and shred them fairly fine. Add to them fresh young peas, tiny green string beans and finely chopped green onions. A few mint leaves and finely chopped parsley may be added. When ready to serve, toss with French dressing to which has been added crumbled blue cheese or shredded cheddar cheese. The amounts to use will depend upon how much you can gather from your garden or from some organic vegetable grower. Serves 4-6.

ITALIAN SALAD

½ cup tarragon vinegar
½ cup salad oil
¾ teaspoon salt
½ teaspoon crushed oregano
  leaves
2 tomatoes peeled and cut
  into chunks

1 cucumber peeled and
  thinly sliced
1 onion sliced and
  separated into rings
¼ cup sliced black olives
¼ cup chopped walnuts
½ cup sliced celery

Combine first four ingredients in covered jar and shake well. Pour over remaining ingredients and toss well. Cover and chill at least 10 minutes, tossing occasionally. Serve on shredded lettuce. Serves 4.

LOW-CALORIE MUSHROOM SALAD

3 cups shredded lettuce
½ pound (2½ cups) fresh,
  sliced mushrooms
½ cucumber, peeled and
  sliced

¼ cup chopped green
  onions
¼ teaspoon oregano
¼ cup French dressing

Combine lettuce, mushrooms, cucumber, onions and oregano in a salad bowl. Pour French salad dressing over all. Toss gently. Serves 6.

ASPARAGUS SALAD

¾ cup oil
½ cup lemon juice
1½ tablespoons honey
1 teaspoon salt or substitute
½ teaspoon tarragon leaves

½ teaspoon thyme leaves
½ teaspoon oregano leaves
½ clove garlic
2 pounds fresh asparagus

Measure oil, lemon juice, honey, salt, tarragon, thyme, oregano into a jar. Add garlic. Cover and shake well. Chill, then remove garlic. Wash and scrape scales from asparagus. Steam only until just tender. Do not

170

overcook. Marinate in the herb dressing you have made for 30 minutes. Remove. Serve on shredded lettuce topped with minced hard-boiled egg. Serves 4. The remaining dressing can be used as a marinade for bean salad or cooked celery salad.

FRESH SPINACH SALAD

¾ pound (about 1 bunch) spinach

6 to 8 ounces fresh bean sprouts, washed

1 small can water chestnuts, sliced

4 thinly sliced green onions

¼ cup each, salad oil, vinegar

2 tablespoons ketchup

Salt and pepper to taste

8 slices bacon, fried and crumbled (optional)

2 hard-boiled eggs, sieved

Remove stems from spinach and discard. Wash leaves and pat dry; break into bit-size pieces. Combine the spinach, bean sprouts, water chestnuts and onions; cover and refrigerate 3 or 4 hours. Mix together salad oil, vinegar and ketchup; salt and pepper to taste. Combine spinach mixture and dressing, mixing carefully. Sprinkle on bacon bits and hard-boiled sieved egg. Serves 4 to 6.

SPROUTED ALFALFA SALAD

1 cup sprouted alfalfa

½ cup green onions chopped

1 cup finely chopped celery

2 avocados, peeled and sliced

1 cup cottage cheese

½ cup minced parsley

Combine sprouts, onion and celery. Arrange on salad plates with avocado slices. Spoon cottage cheese on top of avocado slices and sprinkle parsley on top. Serves 4.

NEW POTATO-ALFALFA SALAD

6 tiny raw new potatoes
  (small cooked new
  potatoes may be used)
1 small can chopped olives
1 chopped onion

1 chopped hard-boiled egg
1 cup alfalfa sprouts
Salt, celery salt and other
  seasonings to taste
Mayonnaise

Wash and scrub potatoes well. If you use cooked potatoes, cook them with jackets on. Cool. Combine with other ingredients. Serve with young, tender celery leaves. Serves 2.

BEAN SPROUT SALAD

4 cups bean sprouts
1 tablespoon chopped
  pimiento
2 tablespoons chopped
  green onion
2 teaspoons sesame seeds

1 clove garlic, minced
1 hard-boiled egg, chopped
2 tablespoons oil
1 tablespoon vinegar
½ teaspoon salt
2 tablespoons soy sauce

Wash bean sprouts and combine with pimiento, green onion, sesame seed, garlic and hard-boiled egg. Combine oil, vinegar, salt and soy sauce. Pour over bean sprout mixture. Toss lightly to coat vegetables well. Chill, garnish with additional egg slices, if desired. Serves 6.

THREE BEAN SALAD

1 cup cooked green beans
1 cup cooked yellow beans
1 cup cooked lima, gar-
  banzo or kidney beans
1 small onion

1 teaspoon salt
½ teaspoon pepper
⅓ cup salad oil
⅔ cup vinegar
Honey to taste

Put beans in a large bowl. Chop onion fine and mix

with beans. In a separate bowl, mix the remaining ingredients.

Pour dressing over bean combination and refrigerate several hours, even overnight, until the vegetables take on the good sour-sweet flavor. Serves 8 to 10.

MARINATED BEAN SALAD

1 package frozen French green beans
1 package frozen wax beans
1 package frozen lima beans
1 4-ounce can mushrooms, drained
½ cup finely chopped onion
2 tablespoons chopped parsley

½ cup wine vinegar (or apple vinegar)
¼ cup olive oil
⅓ cup water
1 clove garlic mashed
¼ teaspoon dried oregano leaves
¼ teaspoon celery salt
½ teaspoon salt
¼ teaspoon pepper

Cook lima beans separately and the other two together. Cool. Combine all vegetables. Place vinegar, oil, water, garlic, oregano, celery salt, salt and pepper in a small jar with a screw top; cover and shake until blended. Pour over vegetables and toss together. Chill in the refrigerator 3 hours or overnight. Serves 8.

CARROT-SESAME SLAW

2 cups grated carrots
2 cups shredded cabbage
1 tablespoon green pepper, chopped
1 tablespoon grated onion

¼ cup sour cream or yogurt
¼ cup mayonnaise
1 teaspoon prepared mustard
1 tablespoon sesame seeds

Toast sesame seeds in a shallow pan in a 350° oven until golden brown. Set aside. In a bowl combine carrots, cabbage, green pepper and grated onion. Blend together sour cream, mayonnaise and mustard. Pour over vegetables and toss lightly. Sprinkle with sesame seeds just before serving. Serves 4.

GRAPE COLE SLAW

3 *cups shredded cabbage*
2 *cups seedless grapes*
1½ *teaspoons salt*
1 *tablespoon lemon juice*
¼ *cup mayonnaise*

Mix ingredients and serve in lettuce cup. Garnish with sliced, seeded red grapes. Serves 6.

APPLE SLAW

1 *small head green cab-bage, grated*
1 *small carrot, grated*
2 *tablespoons celery, chopped*
1 *large apple, grated or chopped*

Dressing: 1 tablespoon honey, ½ teaspoon salt, ¼ teaspoon pepper, 1 tablespoon vinegar and 1 tablespoon mayonnaise. Mix dressing with vegetables and apple, stirring until dressing covers all the salad ingredients. If onion and green pepper are enjoyed, mix in a tablespoon of each. Serves 2 or 3.

CHEESE CARAWAY COLE SLAW

6 *cups shredded cabbage*
1½ *cups shredded cheddar cheese*
½ *teaspoon paprika*
Salt *to taste*
3 *teaspoons vinegar*
1 *teaspoon honey*
1 *cup sour cream or homemade salad dressing*
½ *teaspoon caraway seeds*

With a fork, toss together the shredded cabbage and grated cheese. Combine remaining ingredients and pour over cheese, cabbage salad. Toss lightly and serve immediately. Serves 6.

WATERMELON COMPOTE

1 watermelon half, cut
  lengthwise
1 cup cantaloupe balls
1 cup honeydew chunks

1 cup Persian melon balls
1 cup boysenberries or
  other berries
¼ cup lemon juice

Remove watermelon pulp with a sharp knife and cut into balls with melon ball cutter, flipping out seeds with the tip of a knife. Turn melon shell upside down on paper towels and drain 15 to 20 minutes. If a great deal of liquid collects in melon shell, pour it out and drink it. Cut rim sawtooth fashion if wished. Combine watermelon and cantaloupe balls, honeydew chunks, Persian melon balls, berries and lemon juice and turn into watermelon shell. Chill. Serves 6 to 9.

If you haven't the time to make the above compote, serve cold chilled berries. In buying these berries, look for bright, clean appearance and a uniform good color.

The individual small cells making up the berry should be plump and tender but not mushy. Avoid leaky and moldy berries. You can usually spot them through the openings in the ventilated containers.

Allow a pint of berries for 4 or 5 servings. They should be stored loosely in shallow containers. Wash before using. To keep strawberries several days, do not wash, but place firm berries in a large glass jar with a tight lid; refrigerate until ready to use.

MELON BALL FRUIT CUP

2 cups watermelon balls
2 cups cantaloupe balls
2 tablespoons lemon juice
3 tablespoons honey

1 cup raspberries or blueberries
Fresh mint leaves

Combine watermelon, cantaloupe, berries, lemon juice and honey. Chill at least 1 hour. Serve in sherbet glasses. Garnish with fresh mint leaves. Serves 4.

MAYONNAISE

If you have an electric blender you can make your own mayonnaise in a matter of minutes. Place in blender: 2 tablespoons lemon juice, ½ teaspoon salt, 1 teaspoon prepared mustard, 1 whole egg and ¼ cup oil (olive, or a mixture). Cover, set switch to high. While it is running, remove the cover and very slowly add ¾ cup more oil. It will immediately thicken to a smooth, creamy mayonnaise. This will make 1¼ cupfuls.

ALBERTA SALAD DRESSING

Melt together over a low fire 2 tablespoons bleu cheese and 2 tablespoons sour cream.

Remove from heat and fold in 1 cup sour cream, 2 tablespoons mayonnaise and about ½ cup crumbled bleu cheese. Makes 1½ cups.

Index